Lonely planet

POCKET

COPENHAGEN

TOP EXPERIENCES • LOCAL LIFE

T0018198

EGILL BJARNASON, ABIGAIL BLASI

Contents

Plan Your Trip   4

The Little Mermaid (p83); Sculptor: Edvard Eriksen
SERGII FIGURNYI/SHUTTERSTOCK ©

Welcome to Copenhagen

Calm, cool and collected, Copenhagen has broad cycle lanes busy with commuters, chalky 17th-century houses edging pristine canals and ground-breaking contemporary architecture. Even the street lamps are design classics, and there are creative restaurants, food markets, fabulous museums, the Tivoli theme park, boats, an extraordinary ski slope and a head-spinning amount to do for all ages.

Nyhavn Canal (p77)

Copenhagen's Top Experiences

Enjoy the twinkling wonder of Tivoli Gardens (p42)

MASSIMO PIZZOTTI/SHUTTERSTOCK ©

Relax in Louisiana's Seaside Sculpture Garden (p142)

Learn some Danish history at National-museet (p46)

Admire Danish design at the Design museum (p78)

Wander free-spirited Christiania (p90)

NICK N A/SHUTTERSTOCK ©

Explore Borgen, 'the castle' (p54)

Visit Christian IV's Renaissance castle (p104)

TRABANTOS/SHUTTERSTOCK ©

Explore Denmark's top-tier art museum (p108)

Dining Out

Copenhagen has a glittering array of Michelin-starred restaurants, with Geranium and noma shining brightest. Excellent international restaurants serve authentic dishes like pho, ramen and tacos, while venerable city institutions serve classic Danish fare, including smørrebrød.

Old-School Flavours

Traditional Danish tables are a hearty affair. Pork *(flæskor svinekød)* dominates in comfort-food favourite *frikadeller,* (pictured) fried minced-pork meatballs commonly served with boiled potatoes and red cabbage. Equally iconic is the majestic *stjerneskud*. Literally 'shooting star', it's a belt-busting combination of steamed and fried fish fillets, topped with smoked salmon, shrimp and caviar, and served on buttered bread.

The Sweet Stuff

Ironically, what is known as a 'Danish pastry' abroad is here called a *wienerbrød* (Viennese bread), due to the influence of Viennese bakers in the 19th century. Made from layers of buttery pastry, local favourites include *kanelsnegle* (cinnamon snail), and *spandauer*, cream or fruit encircled by pastry (named after Berlin's Spandau prison).

Best Traditional Danish

Schønnemann Epic repertoire of smørrebrød. (p70)

Orangeriet Lunchtime smørrebrød in a romantic garden setting. (p105)

Kanal Caféen Glorious Danish platters and a canal-side location. (p50)

Best Modern Danish

noma René Redzepi–founded New Nordic icon. (p99)

Kadeau Breathtakingly creative degustation. (p98)

Høst Sophisticated New Nordic at approachable prices. (p114)

Restaurant Mes Subtle foreign twists and whimsical presentation. (p49)

Aamanns 1921 Beautiful, taste-sensation smørrebrød. (p70)

SERGII KOVAL/SHUTTERSTOCK ©

Pluto Seasonal, honest grub in a convivial space. (p114)

Best Seafood

Silberbauers Bistro Oysters and shellfish at a casual favourite. (p121)

Kødbyens Fiskebar Creative sharing plates; buzzy industrial setting. (p136)

Best Asian Flavours

District Tonkin Authentic banh mi and northern Vietnamese bites. (p84)

The Market Intriguing pan-Asian flavours in a slinky space. (p70)

Best Southern European

Bæst Italo-Danish artisan cheeses, charcuterie and wood-fired pizzas. (p121)

A Terre High-end French cuisine; sophisticated dining room. (p84)

Fischer Exquisite antipasti and pasta in a low-key bistro. (p127)

Best Cheap Eats

Hija de Sanchez Real-deal tacos from a noma alumnus. (p136)

Gasoline Grill Juicy organic burgers in Norrebrø. (p114)

Morgenstedet Organic vegetarian in a bucolic Christiania setting. (p98)

DØP Premium dogs made with 100% organic ingredients. (p71)

Top Tips

○ Book at popular restaurants, especially later in the week.

○ Locals don't eat out late: dining after 10pm will be tricky.

Treasure Hunt

This is Danish design nirvana, Scandinavia's capital of cool, with myriad locally designed and crafted must-haves. Good buys that are easy to carry home include ceramics, glassware, jewellery and textiles. Pre-Christmas, you can buy whimsical decorations galore, especially nisse (gnomes) and candles. Ready, set, shop.

Where to Shop

Strøget has high-street shops, with more upmarket options at its eastern end (Østergade). Amagertorv is home to Royal Copenhagen, George Jensen and design behemoth Illums Bolighus (p73). More chains line Købmagergade, with the hippest Nordic fashion stores east of Købmagergade and north of Østergade. A few vintage stores dot the Latin Quarter, with quirky, higher-end fashion stops on Krystalgade.

North of Nyhavn, Bredgade offers exclusive art and antiques. For independent shops and bric-a-brac, vintage jewellery and kitsch, scour Ravnsborggade, Elmegade and Jægersborggade in Nørrebro or Nørrebro Loppemarked, the seasonal Saturday flea market. Frederiksberg Bredegade also has an excellent Saturday flea market.

Vesterbro has some good independent fashion and home-wares, especially Istedgade and Værndamsvej.

Best for Womenswear

Stine Goya Playful, individualistic outfits from Denmark's hottest independent designer. (p115)

Baum und Pferdgarten Bold, colourful, higher-end collections from a Danish duo. (p75)

Storm Harder-to-find labels, accessories and gifts. (p75)

Best for Menswear

Samsøe & Samsøe Supercool, comfy casualwear from Samsøe and guest labels. (p131)

Magasin du Nord Department store sees lots of local labels in one place. (p75)

HEMIS/ALAMYSTOCKPHOTO ©

Best for Interior Design

Hay House Contemporary furniture, furnishings and gifts from new-school Scandi talent. (p73)

Illums Bolighus Four floors of design porn. (pictured; p73)

Magasin du Nord Great designer homewares with many smaller Danish labels. (p75)

Best Gourmet Treats

Torvehallerne KBH Heaves with goods for the pantry and cellar. (p110)

Juuls Vin og Spiritus Stock the cellar with Nordic akvavits, gins and more. (p131)

Best Local Gifts & Souvenirs

Designmuseum Danmark Cool, easy-to-carry gifts. (p78)

Ny Carlsberg Glyptotek Magnificent museum shop with lovely museum-based souvenirs. (p49)

Dansk Arkitektur Center Architecturally themed ephemera and quirky gifts in the BLOX basement. (p61)

Tivoli Gardens Craft stalls sell gloves, sheepskins and Tivoli mugs full of mulled wine in winter – pay extra and keep the mug. (p42)

Gågrøn! Eco-friendly Danish gifts: organic skincare, snug knits, quirky glassware and ceramics. (p125)

Top Tip

Refund Scheme Non-EU citizens can claim a VAT refund as they leave the EU. Spend at least 300kr at shops that participate in the refund scheme. Ask the shop to fill in a refund form. Present it at the airport with your passport, receipts and purchases.

Museums & Galleries

Copenhagen's eclectic, dazzling museums house cultural treasures like ancient tomb wares and sacrificial bodies, swords and jewels, iconic modernist design and contemporary installations.

Plan Your Visit

Many museums and galleries close at least one day a week, usually Monday. Some stay open late one or more nights a week, often Wednesday or Thursday. Some museums – among them Ny Carlsberg Glyptotek and Thorvaldsens Museum – offer free admission once a week, often Wednesday or Sunday.

Park Museums

Statens Museum for Kunst, Rosenborg Slot, Davids Samling, Hirschsprung, Statens Naturhistoriske Museum (including Geologisk Museum) and Arbejdermuseet together form the **Parkmuseerne** (www. parkmuseerne.dk) district. A combination ticket covers all venues and includes a 10% discount at museum stores.

Best for History

Nationalmuseet Remarkable artefacts spanning the country's biography, plus a children's wing. (p46)

Frihedsmuseet Vividly evokes life during the Danish WWII resistance. (p82)

Museum of Copenhagen Creative interactive displays take you through the development of Copenhagen. (p49)

Rosenborg Slot Royal bling in Christian IV's Renaissance summer pad. (pictured; p104)

Ruinerne under Christiansborg Ruins of Copenhagen's earliest fortress and castle. (p55)

Designmuseum Danmark Explore the roots of Danish design. (p78)

Best Art Museums

Statens Museum for Kunst Denmark's preeminent art collection spans medieval to modern. (p108)

Louisiana Masterpieces and modernism, in a glorious waterfront location. (p142)

DIEGO GRANDI/SHUTTERSTOCK ©

Ny Carlsberg Glyptotek
Egyptian and Mediterranean antiquities plus Impressionist art. (p49)

Thorvaldsens Museum
Building designed to complement nation's greatest sculptor. (p61)

Best Lesser-known Treasures

Copenhill Out-there ski slope with big views, atop a waste-treatment power plant. (p95)

Hirschsprung An elegant repository of 19th- and 20th-century Danish art. (p113)

Dansk Jødisk Museum
Jewry heritage in a space designed by architect Daniel Libeskind. (p62)

Frihedsmuseet Contemporary foray into the Danish WWII resistance. (p82)

Best Contemporary Art Galleries

Kunsthal Charlottenborg
One of Europe's largest venues for modern talent from around the globe. (p84)

Kunstforeningen GL Strand Canal-side showcase of forward-thinking local and foreign works. (p69)

V1 Gallery Edgy exhibitions in Vesterbro's vibrant Meatpacking District. (p134)

Cisternerne A former underground reservoir turned dramatic installation space. (p141)

Top Tip

Copenhagen Card (www.copenhagencard.com) offers free entry to over 80 museums and attractions, and free public transport. Sights include Rosenborg Slot, Nationalmuseet and Ny Carlsberg Glyptotek. Buy it at the airport tourist office, saving the need to buy an onward train or metro ticket.

Under the Radar Copenhagen

Head off the beaten track and your reward is a more genuine slice of Copenhagen life, one filled with unique neighbourhoods, artisan studios and tranquil gardens made for perfect picnics.

Local Neighbourhoods

Exploring less-touristed neighbourhoods allows you to tap into the city the locals know, to better understand Copenhagen, its people and nuances, and to support smaller neighbourhood businesses.

Multicultural **Nørrebro** is home to some 60 different nationalities, not to mention a large community of artists and students. Streets like Jægersborggade,

Blågårdsgade and Elmegade buzz with independent boutiques, galleries, restaurants, cafes and bars. At the northern end of Nørrebrogade (Nørrebro's main thoroughfare) is Superkilen (p121), an imaginative, one-of-a-kind park celebrating the neighbourhood's diversity.

In chi-chi **Østerbro**, colourful Brumleby and Olufsvej are gorgeous heritage areas, while leafy, cafe-flanked Bopa Plads (Bopa Sq) is a popular hangout for Østerbro locals.

Beyond Kødbyen (Meatpacking District) in **Vesterbro**, make time to explore the neighbourhood's village-like Værnedamsvej, as well as Vesterbro's giant street-art murals.

West of Vesterbro lies salubrious **Frederiksberg** (pictured), home to romantic Frederiksberg Have, the extraordinary subterranean art-gallery Cisternerne and cult-status flea market Frederiksberg Loppetorv.

ASMUS KOEFOED/SHUTTERSTOCK ©

Best Off-Track Sights

Davids Samling Superb Islamic and European art, hidden away in a collector's former townhouse. (p113)

Assistens Kirkegård Burial place of Hans Christian Andersen and a much-loved picnic spot. (p121)

Cisternerne Moody, subterranean reservoir turned contemporary art space in Frederiksberg. (p141)

Best Neighbourhood Shopping

Vanishing Point Thoughtfully curated local crafts and gifts, from quirky ceramics to hand-knitted sweaters. (p125)

Gågrøn! Useful, sustainable Danish items like organic soaps, candles and biodynamic woollen socks. (p125)

Frederiksberg Loppetorv Frederiksberg's Saturday flea market draws curious locals and serious collectors alike. (p141)

Best Neighbourhood Hangouts

Palæ Bar Smoky, old-school bodega where seasoned regulars drink, play chess and tap fingertips to jazz. (p73)

Brus Cult-status craft beers and superb bites in a big, old Nørrebro factory. (p123)

Pixie Quintessential neighbourhood cafe-bar, on a leafy Østerbro square. (p127)

Lille Bakery Destination baked delights in Refshaleøen. (p95)

Bar Open

Copenhagen's vibrant drinking areas include Vesterbro's Kødbyen (Meatpacking District), Istedgade and the northern end of Viktoriagade; Nørrebro's Ravnsborggade, Elmegade, Sankt Hans Torv and Jægersborggade; and the historic Latin Quarter.

A is for Akvavit

Denmark's most popular spirit is the Aalborg-produced akvavit. There are several dozen types, the most common of which is made from potatoes and spiced with caraway seeds. In Denmark akvavit is not sipped but is swallowed straight down as a shot, usually followed by a chaser of *øl* (beer).

It's Øl Good

Copenhagen's first brewing guild was established in 1525. Its homegrown breweries include commercial giant Carlsberg and craft-brewer Mikkeller. The latter is one of several independents producing innovative beers in a variety of styles.

While the best-selling beers in Denmark are pilsners, a lager with an alcohol content of 4.6%, there are scores of beers to choose from. These range from light beers with an alcohol content of 1.7% to hearty stouts that kick in at 8%. Thirsty? Remember these handy terms: *lyst øl* (light beer), *lagerøl* (dark lager), *fadøl* (draught), *porter* (stout) and *bryghus* (brewery or brewpub).

Best for Cocktails

Ruby Meticulous, made-from-scratch cocktails at a world-renowned bar. (p72)

Lidkoeb Beautiful libations in a hidden location right off Vesterbrogade. (p137)

1105 A dark, sleek city-centre cocktail den for grown-ups. (p72)

Best for Wine

Ved Stranden 10 Knowledgeable staff pouring unusual drops. (p71)

Nebbiolo Trendy Italian enoteca with top drops just off Nyhavn. (p86)

RADIOKAFKA/SHUTTERSTOCK ©

Nebbiolo Antipasti Natural wines with fine-dining antipasti. (p86)

Den Vandrette Natural wines and summertime harbourside tables. (p86)

Falernum Wines by the glass on a Parisian-esque Vesterbro strip. (p131)

Best for Craft Beer

Fermentoren Cosy, candlelit basement, with a wide range on tap. (p138)

Mikkeller & Friends Craft brews, plus Belgian-style beers in a back bar. (pictured; p124)

Nørrebro Bryghus Organic craft beers from a maverick urban micro-brewery. (p125)

Best for Coffee

Coffee Collective Copenhagen's most revered specialty micro-roastery. (p124)

Sort Kaffe & Vinyl Record store and coffee shop in ever-hip Vesterbro. (p138)

Democratic Coffee Smooth specialty brews in the erudite Latin Quarter. (p73)

Best for a View

Kayak Bar Waterfront bar for laidback drinks. (p63)

Illum Rooftop City views from the rooftop restaurants and cafe. (p73)

La Banchina Harbour cove with picnic tables and a wooden pier. (p95)

Seaside Toldboden Waterside bar in the former Customs House turned gastronomic complex. (p85)

Nyhavn For Less

Skip Nyhavn's touristy canal-side bars and buy your drinks more cheaply at convenience store Turs Havneproviant on nearby Lille Strandstræde 3. Stocked up, enjoy your canal-side tipple; it's legal.

Showtime

AGEHRIG/SHUTTERSTOCK © ARCHITECT: HENNING LARSEN

Copenhagen's entertainment offerings are wide, varied and sophisticated. On any given night choices will include ballet, opera, theatre, clubbing and live gigs. The city has a world-renowned jazz scene, with numerous jazz clubs drawing top talent. Note: many night-spots don't get the party started until 11pm or midnight.

Best Live Music & DJs

Vega Three venues in one, serving up an alphabet of genres. (p138)

Culture Box Electronic music spun by A-list local and global DJs. (p115)

Loppen Raw, feverish, alternative acts in a scruffy Christiania warehouse. (p93)

Best Jazz & Blues

Blågårds Apotek A former pharmacy renowned for weekly jazz. (p122)

Jazzhus Montmartre A veteran jazz peddler, with decent pre-show dining. (p73)

Mojo Moody nightly tunes spanning blues to soul,

plus an affable, welcoming vibe. (p51)

Best Performing Arts

Det Kongelige Teater Encore-worthy ballet and opera in Copenhagen's most opulent period theatre. (p86)

Skuespilhuset Contemporary home of the Royal Danish Theatre, with classic and modern productions. (p87)

Operæn Sterling opera in a show-stopping harbourside landmark. (pictured; p101)

Best for Cinephiles

Cinemateket Independent cinema with bimonthly Danish film classics. (p73)

Grand Teatret A vintage movie house with a weakness for Euro movies. (p51)

Top Tip

Tivoli Gardens box office (☎33 15 10 01; https://www.tivoli.dk/en/praktisk) sells tickets for Tivoli performances and is also an agent for **Ticketmaster** (☎70 15 65 65; www.ticketmaster.dk), which sells tickets for concerts, theatre, sport and more.

For Free

While Copenhagen is hardly a bargain destination, some of its most impressive sights are always free, while others are free on specific days of the week. Best of all the city's compact size means it's easy enough to cover much on foot or by bike, keeping costs lower and your spirits higher.

ARTMEDIAFACTORY/SHUTTERSTOCK ©

Best Free Museums

Davids Samling European paintings, Islamic treasures and applied arts; always free. (p113)

Ny Carlsberg Glyptotek From Egyptian tombs to French Impressionists; free on Tuesdays. (p49)

Thorvaldsens Museum Ode to Denmark's most accomplished sculptor; free on Wednesdays. (p61)

Nikolaj Kunsthal Contemporary art exhibitions at a former church; free on Wednesdays. (pictured; p69)

Museum of Copenhagen Town history; free on Fridays. (p49)

Best Free Experiences

Nyhavn Candy-coloured 17th-century harbour. (p82)

Black Diamond Stupendous interiors and views at Copenhagen's contemporary library wing. (p61)

Assistens Kirkegård One-on-one time with some of Denmark's most illustrious historical figures. (p121)

Islands Brygge Havne-badet Glorious harbour pool complex. (p98)

Christiania Copenhagen's most unconventional neighbourhood. (p90)

Christiansborg Slot Tower Views from Copenhagen's tallest tower. (p56)

Botanisk Have Denmark's largest collection of living plants. (p113)

Top Tip

Copenhagen Free Walking Tours (www.copenhagen freewalkingtours.dk) runs a three-hour Grand Tour of Copenhagen, departing from outside Rådhus; and a 90-minute Christianshavn tour departing from Højbro Plads, both several times weekly. A tip is expected; see the website for times.

Tours

JONATHAN SMITH/LONELY PLANET ©

Best Overview Tours

Netto-Bådene (www. havnerundfart.dk) The cheapest of Copenhagen's harbour and canal tours, with embarkation points at Holmens Kirke and Nyhavn (pictured).

Stromma (www. stromma.dk; Nyhavn) Popular one-hour harbour and canal tours departing from Nyhavn and Ved Stranden, plus hop-on, hop-off bus tours, or a combo of the two.

Best Active Tours

Kayak Republic (www. kayakrepublic.dk) Two-hour tours along the city's canals, as well as evening paddles to catch the sunset. Located just beside Christian IV's Bro.

Bike Copenhagen With Mike (www.bikecopen hagenwithmike.dk) Idiosyncratic, fun cycling tours of Copenhagen, departing from Sankt Peders Stræde 47 in the city centre. Dining and private tours are also available; see the website.

Running Tours Copenhagen (www.runningtours. dk) Raise your pulse while you jog through the city and its history. Tours commence in Rådhuspladsen.

Best Themed Tours

Nordic Noir Tours (www.nordicnoirtours. com) Retrace the steps of your favourite Nordic TV characters from *Borgen*, *The Bridge* and *The Killing* on these 90-minute location walking tours.

CPH:cool (www.cphcool. dk) Two- and 2½-hour insider walking tours with themes like shopping, architecture, design, gastronomy and beer. Tours leave from outside the Copenhagen Visitors Centre.

For Kids

ABIGAIL BLASI ©

Copenhagen's design ethic encompasses family life, with loads of thoughtful things for kids to do. There's free entry for under 18s at most museums.

Don't Miss

Hands-on science museum **Experimentarium** (www.experimentarium.dk/en) and the national aquarium **Den Blå Planet** (www.denblaaplanet.dk) which is one metro stop from the airport.

Best Art, Science & Nature

Dansk Arkitektur Center Carsten Höller slide; interactive exhibitions. (p61)

Statens Museum for Kunst Sketching, workshops, monthly kids' day. (p108)

Louisiana Huge children's wing and a garden. (p142)

Copenhagen Zoo Polar bears and pandas. (p141)

Best Outdoor Thrills

Tivoli Gardens Charming amusement park. (p42)

Copenhill Skiing and rock-climbing at a working powerplant. (p95)

Islands Brygge Havnebadet The city's favourite harbour pool. (pictured; p98)

GoBoat Play 'trash pirates' on solar boats. (p99)

Kongens Have Catch a summer puppet show. (p107)

Best Historical Insight

Nationalmuseet Be a Viking, knight, schoolteacher and shopkeeper. (p46)

Museum of Copenhagen State-of-the-art interactive history. (p49)

Rosenborg Slot Gingerbread-style castle. (p104)

Top Tips

○ Larger bike-hire outfits have kids' or Christiania bikes with passenger trailers.

○ Kids aged 12 to 15 pay half price on public transport. An adult with a valid ticket can take two under 12s for free.

LGBTIQ+

In 1989, Denmark was the first country to allow same-sex couples to register as domestic partners, and the country has long been a beacon of queer inclusivity. Copenhagen is one of the world's friendliest LGBTIQ+ cities, with an open, thriving and integrated community.

ANDRIJ VATSYK/SHUTTERSTOCK ©

LGBTIQ+ Areas

There's not a specific area in Copenhagen; rather, the whole city is Scandinavia's LGBTIQ+ centre. Most clubs and bars are located in the Latin Quarter and just off Rådhuspladsen in the city centre.

Best Bars

Centralhjørnet (www. centralhjornet.dk) Open since 1917, this is an historic gay bar.

Vela Gay Club (www. velagayclub.dk) Long-running lesbian bar.

Best Events

Copenhagen Pride Week (www.copenhagen pride.dk; ☺Feb & Aug; pictured).

MIX Copenhagen (www. mixcopenhagen.dk; ☺late Oct).

Winter Pride (www.copen hagenpride.dk; ☺first week of Feb).

Architecture

Copenhagen's architectural cache is rich and diverse, spanning many centuries and architectural styles. This is a city with a contemporary edge, its Renaissance, baroque and National Romantic treasures sharing the spotlight with modernist icons and innovative marvels that inspire urban planners across the globe.

VLADIMIR MUCIBABIC/SHUTTERSTOCK ©
ARCHITECT: SCHMIDT HAMMER LASSEN ARCHITECTS ©

Historical Overview

Copenhagen's architectural legacy begins with Bishop Absalon's 12th-century fortress, its ruins visible beneath Christiansborg Slot. 'Builder King' Christian IV embarked on an extraordinary building program in the 17th century that includes Børsen, Rundetårn and Rosenborg Slot. Rococo delights include Amalienborg Slot and Marmorkirken, while Rådhus (City Hall) is a standout example of the 19th-century National Romantic style.

Rosenborg Slot A petite castle built in the Dutch Renaissance style. (p104)

Christiansborg Slot Copenhagen's boldest Neo-Baroque statement. (p54)

Rundetårn Christian IV's astronomical tower, complete with equestrian staircase. (p68)

Børsen A Dutch Renaissance stock exchange with rooftop dragons. (p61)

Det Kongelige Bibliotek The 'Black Diamond' heralded a new era for Copenhagen's waterfront. (pictured; p61)

Operæn Copenhagen's harbourfront opera house divides opinion. (p101)

Top Tip

The **Dansk Arkitektur Center** (p61) in Dutch architect Rem Koolhaas' Lego-like BLOX building, has interactive exhibitions, a Carsten Höller slide, a cafe and a bookshop. It also runs architecture walking tours.

Danish Design

Is there a more design-obsessed capital than Copenhagen? In Denmark design excellence is in the DNA. From its restaurant and hotel interiors to its cycling overpasses, one of Copenhagen's most inspirational qualities is its love and mastery of the applied arts.

Y.LEVY/ALAMYSTOCKPHOTO ©

Kaare Klint: Danish Design Pioneer

Modern Danish design bloomed in the '50s but its roots are in the '20s and the work of Danish modernist Kaare Klint (1888–1954). The architect spent much of his career studying the human form and he modified chair designs for added functionality. Klint's obsession with functionality, accessibility and detail would ultimately drive and define Denmark's mid-20th-century design scene and broader design legacy.

Best for Design

Klassik Moderne Møbelkunst Retail repository for the country's most celebrated chairs, tables and more. (p87)

Høst The urban-rustic interior of this New Nordic nosh spot has swagged international awards. (p114)

Designmuseum Danmark Design heritage history and iconic pieces. (p78)

Hay House Furniture, homewares and gifts from new-school Nordic talent. (pictured; p73)

Illums Bolighus Biggest design names on four levels. (p73)

Dansk Arkitektur Center Exhibitions on architecture and urban design. (p61)

Top Tip

The annual **3 Days of Design** (www.3daysofdesign.dk) festival sees dozens of venues, such as furniture and design stores, cafes and Designmuseum Danmark, host special design-themed events.

Festivals & Events

Bass-thumping block parties and saxy jazz, pot-stirring celebrity chefs, groundbreaking films and documentaries, and a rainbow-coloured Pride parade: Copenhagen's social calendar is a buzz-inducing, toe-tapping affair. Sunshine, sleet or snow, you're bound to find a reason to head out and celebrate the finer things in life.

OLIVER FOERSTNER/SHUTTERSTOCK ©

Best for Culture Vultures

Kulturnatten (Culture Night; www.kulturnatten.dk) Late-night art and culture, usually in mid-October.

Kulturhavn (www.kulturhavn.kk.dk/en) Three days of mostly free harbourside events in August.

Best for Music

Copenhagen Jazz Festival (www.jazz.dk) Over three weeks of world-class jazz in July. A winter edition is held in February. (pictured)

Copenhagen Blues Festival (www.copen hagenbluesfestival.dk) Three days of international blues in late September or early October.

Strøm (www.stromcph.dk) A four-day electronic music festival in August.

Distortion (www.cphdis tortion.dk) Five heady days of club and block parties in late May or early June.

Best for Foodies

Copenhagen Cooking (www.copenhagencooking.dk) Scandinavia's largest food festival in August.

Copenhagen Beer Week (www.thefoodproject.dk) Showcases Danish brewers over nine days in September.

Top Tip

The best source of up-to-date info on events is **VisitCopenhagen** (www.visit copenhagen.com). Also useful is the English-language **Copenhagen Post** (www.cphpost.dk).

Responsible Travel

Positive, sustainable and feel-good experiences around the city.

Dos and Don'ts

Don't swim in the wrong place. There are several harbour baths designated for swimming, which are very popular when the weather is warm enough, and Copenhagen is justly renowned for its clean canals. However, you should not swim outside the special swimming areas, which can be risky both because of water quality and traffic.

Do reduce waste. Refill your water bottle at one of the city's 60-plus drinking fountains; the local water is fresh and clean.

Do be on time. It's considered impolite not to be punctual in Denmark, so don't be late!

On the Road

Travel off-season. Book a visit outside summer months (mid-June to August) and Christmas, and midweek instead of weekends.

Do as the Copenhageners do and get around town on a bike. The city's cycling network is the world's best and bike rental is widely available. This includes public bike-sharing scheme **Bycyklen** (https://bycyklen.dk/.

Use clear hand signals when cycling. Raise your hand when you are coming to a stop.

Cycle considerately. Always use the cycle lanes when available and don't cycle on the pavement. Use lights at night, and move to the right to make room for

another cyclist who indicates they want to overtake.

Don't disregard traffic lights. Danes, whether driving, cycling or walking, obey the traffic signals and don't cross when it's red.

Give Back

Consider volunteering. There is less opportunity for people without knowledge of Danish, but a good place to check is www.volunteering.dk, which tries to bring organisations and volunteers with international backgrounds together.

Support Local

Stay in a hotel. Consider ditching apartment lets for a hotel; not only do the latter support local jobs and help

WILLIAM PERUGINI/SHUTTERSTOCK ©

prevent long-term soaring rents for locals, most hotel rooms in Copenhagen hold an official eco-certification.

Resources

Check **VisitCopenhagen** (visitcopenhagen.com) and **VisitDenmark** (visit denmark.com) for tips and resources on responsible, sustainable travel in the city.

Climate Change & Travel

It's impossible to ignore the impact we have when travelling, and the importance of making changes where we can.

Lonely Planet urges all travellers to engage with their travel carbon footprint. There are many carbon calculators online that allow travellers to estimate the carbon emissions generated by their journey; try resurgence.org/resources/carbon-calculator.html. Many airlines and booking sites offer travellers the option of offsetting the impact of greenhouse gas emissions by contributing to climate-friendly initiatives around the world.

We continue to offset the carbon foot-print of all Lonely Planet staff travel, while recognising this is a mitigation more than a solution.

Four Perfect Days

Day One

ALEXANDERSTOCK23/SHUTTERSTOCK ©

Pique your appetite at food market **Torvehallerne KBH** (pictured above; p110). Walk over to **Kongens Have** (p107), royal backyard turned city park, and snoop around its 17th-century castle, **Rosenborg Slot** (p104).

Continue east to rainbow-bright harbour **Nyhavn** (p82), then hop on a canal-and-harbour tour of the city (p24). Alternatively, head to royal pad **Amalienborg Slot** (p82), the glorious **Marmorkirken** (p83) and the **Designmuseum** (p78). The **Little Mermaid** (p83) awaits nearby.

Spend the evening at **Tivoli Gardens** (p42). If it's Friday night, you might catch one of Tivoli's gigs.

Day Two

PAPARAZZA/SHUTTERSTOCK ©

Start on a high by climbing **Rundetårn** (p68), a 17th-century tower with views. The streets to the east are dotted with Nordic fashion boutiques, and to the southwest is the historic **Latin Quarter** (p68). It's here that you'll find **Vor Frue Kirke** (pictured above; p68), home to sculptures by Bertel Thorvaldsen.

You could easily spend the afternoon exploring Danish history at the **Nationalmuseet** (p46), followed by Egyptian sarcophagi and impressionist painting at **Ny Carlsberg Glyptotek** (p49).

Continue the night at **Ved Stranden 10** (p71), **Ruby** (p72) or **Jazzhus Montmartre** (p73).

Day Three

SAMNATA/SHUTTERSTOCK ©

Spend the morning exploring Christianshavn (p89). If it's open, pop into theatrical **Christians Kirke** (p98). Architectural curiosity also underscores **Vor Frelsers Kirke** (p97). Both are in walking distance of **Christiania** (pictured above; p90).

After lunch, cross Knippelsbro (Knippels Bridge) to reach Slotsholmen. The island's protagonist is **Christiansborg Slot** (p54), but don't neglect to see **Dansk Arkitektur Center,** (p61) the **Black Diamond** (p61) and **Thorvaldsens Museum** (p61).

Kick back in Kødbyen, the city's on-trend 'Meatpacking District', and finish at a bar such as **Mesteren & Lærlingen** (p138), craft-beer standout **Mikkeller Bar** (p137) or cocktail hideout **Lidkoeb** (p137).

Day Four

RADIOKAFA/SHUTTERSTOCK ©

Delve into masterpieces both old and cutting edge at **Statens Museum for Kunst** (p108), Denmark's national gallery, with its superb Matisse collection. The canvas-worthy **Botanisk Have** (p113) is across the road.

In the afternoon continue the art theme by heading to Copen-hagen's **Louisiana Museum of Modern Art** (p142), one of the world's great art galleries, not only for its modernist master-pieces, but also for its seaside sculpture garden.

Spend the evening exploring Nørrebro, with its plethora of idi-osyncratic drinking holes, among them craft-beer hotspots **Brus** (p123) and **Mikkeller & Friends** (pictured above: p124) or the soulful **Kind of Blue** (p125).

Need to Know

For detailed information, see Survival Guide (p145)

Language
Danish; English widely spoken

Currency
Danish krone (kr)

Visas
No visa required for EU and Schengen countries, or for tourist stays of less than 90 days for UK, USA, Canada, Australia, New Zealand, most Latin American and some Asian countries. (p151)

Money
ATMs widely available. Credit cards accepted in most places.

Mobile Phones
Mobile coverage is widespread. Non-EU residents should bring a GSM-compatible phone; local SIM cards are available.

Time
Central European Time

Tipping
Tip 10% of the bill for exceptional service at restaurants and round up the fare in taxis.

Daily Budget

Budget: Less than 1000kr

Dorm bed: 200–300kr

Double room in budget hotel: 600–800kr

Cheap meal: under 150kr

Midrange: 1000–1500kr

Double room in midrange hotel: 900–1700kr

Museum admission: 50–150kr

Three-course menu 350-450kr

Top end: More than 1500kr

Double room in top-end hotel: 4500kr and up

Degustation menu at Kadeau: 2950kr

Advance Planning

Two months before Book your hotel and a table at top restaurants.

One to two weeks before Secure a table at hotspot restaurants.

Few days before Scan www.visit copenhagen.com and www.aok.dk for upcoming events.

Arriving in Copenhagen

Arrival is by air to Copenhagen Airport, train to Central Station, long-distance bus or by ferry.

✈ Copenhagen Airport

Trains run to the centre every 10 to 20 minutes (fewer overnight). Metro is 24/7 (every four to 20 minutes). Taxis to the centre cost 250kr to 300kr. Copenhagen doesn't have ride-sharing apps.

🚌 Central Station

All regional and international trains arrive at and depart from Central Station (København H) in the city centre. Most long-distance buses terminate at Ingerslevsgade, at the southern end of Central Station.

⚓ DFDS Terminal

Cruise ferries to/from Norway and Sweden dock at DFDS Terminal (Søndre Frihavn). Get a shuttle bus or No 27 to the centre.

Getting Around

Copenhagen has an excellent metro, train, bus and ferry network.

🚲 Bike

Copenhagen is flat, bike-friendly and has broad cycle lanes. Bike rental is widely available.

🚌 Bus

Primary routes have an 'A' after the route number and run 24 hours. Night buses (N) run 1am to 5am.

Ⓜ Metro

Four 24-hour lines: M1, M2, M3 and M4. M2 runs to the airport (12 minutes from Kongens Nytorv).

🚌 Train

Seven suburban lines (S-tog) run via Central Station. All-night services on Fridays and Saturdays.

⚓ Ferry

There are nine commuter-ferry (harbour-bus) stops. Havnebus 991 goes south and 992 north.

For much more on getting around, see p147.

Useful Websites

Lonely Planet (lonelyplanet.com/denmark/copenhagen) Intel, bookings and more.

Rejseplanen (www.rejseplanen.dk) Useful journey planner.

Visit Copenhagen (www.visitcopenhagen.com) Accommodation and up-to-date information.

Copenhagen Neighbourhoods

Nørrebro (p117)
Copenhagen at its graffiti-scrawled best, jam-packed with indie cafes, rocking retro treasures and buried national legends.

Nørreport (p103)
An appetite-piquing, soul-stirring feast of market produce, artistic masterpieces, royal turrets and jewels, and dashing parklands.

Vesterbro (p129)
The pinnacle of Copenhagen cool, where post-industrial bars, eateries and galleries mix with vintage second-hand shops.

Tivoli
Gardens

Nyhavn & the Royal Quarter (p77)
Masts and maritime buildings, a rococo royal palace and the world's most famous mermaid – welcome to the city of postcard images.

Strøget & Around (p65)
Nordic fashion flagships, buzzing cafes and bars, and twisting cobbled streets draw the crowds to Copenhagen's historic heart.

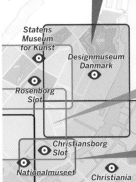

Statens Museum for Kunst

Designmuseum Danmark

Rosenborg Slot

Christiansborg Slot

Nationalmuseet

Christiania

Slotsholmen (p53)
Parliamentary palace, medieval ruins, blue-blooded artefacts and a gobsmacking library: tiny Slotsholmen packs a powerful punch.

Tivoli Area (p41)
Copenhagen's bustling 'welcome mat', home to the cultural blockbuster Nationalmuseet and whimsical wonderland Tivoli Gardens.

Christianshavn (p89)
Scandinavia's answer to Amsterdam, pimped with cosy canals, boats and cafes, and the pot-scented streets of alt-living commune Christiania.

Explore
Copenhagen

Worth a Trip 👓

Copenhagen's Walking Tours 🚶

Panorama of Copenhagen SERGII FIGURNYI/SHUTTERSTOCK ©

Explore ⊕
Tivoli Area

The wonderful whimsy of Copenhagen's unusually beautiful amusement park, Tivoli Gardens, dominates the city centre, across from Central Station and facing the main tourist office. Just across the road is Rådhuspladsen (City Hall Sq), whose design is inspired by the Palio, the famous piazza in Siena, Italy, which was based on a seashell.

The Short List

○ **Tivoli Gardens (p42)** *Enter a wonderland of gleeful rides, storybook pavilions, live music and dance.*

○ **Nationalmuseet (p46)** *Eye up ancient bog bodies and Viking treasures on a trip through Danish history.*

○ **Ny Carlsberg Glyptotek (p49)** *Muse on Mediterranean antiquities and European masterpieces.*

○ **Rådhus (p49)** *Hit Copenhagen's ornate City Hall for its interiors, timepiece and dizzying rooftop views.*

○ **Restaurant Mes (p49)** *Book a table at one of the capital's most impressive contemporary restaurants.*

Getting There & Around

🚌 Most routes stop at Central Station or Rådhuspladsen. Routes 6A and 26 reach Frederiksberg Have via Vesterbro. Route 1A connects Slotsholmen, Nyhavn, the Royal Quarter and Østerbro. Routes 2A and 37 reach Christianshavn.

🚆 All S-train lines stop at Central Station and Vesterport, serving destinations such as the airport and Louisiana.

Tivoli Area Map on p48

Ny Carlsberg Glyptotek (p49) OLIVER FOERSTNER/SHUTTERSTOCK ©

Top Experience 📷

Enjoy the Twinkling Wonder of Tivoli Gardens

Full of vintage charm, wandering peacocks and fanciful architecture, Tivoli Gardens is the world's second-oldest amusement park, opening in 1843. Walt Disney visited for inspiration in 1951, opening Disneyland four years later. Events change in line with the seasons: outdoor ballet in summer, Halloween displays in autumn, and Christmas stalls, decorations and mulled wine in winter.

◉ MAP P48, A4

www.tivoligardens.com

Star Flyer

The Star Flyer will have you twirling around at heights of up to 80m. It's a bit like being on a skyscraping swing, travelling at 70km/h and taking in breathtaking views of Copenhagen's historical towers and rooftops. The astrological symbols, quadrants and planets on the ride are a tribute of sorts to Danish astronomer Tycho Brahe.

Roller Coasters

Rutschebanen (The Roller Coaster) is the best loved of Tivoli's roller coasters, rollicking through and around a faux 'mountain' and reaching speeds of 60km/h. Built in 1914, it claims to be the world's oldest operating wooden roller coaster. If you're hankering for something more hardcore, jump on the Dæmonen (The Demon), a 21st-century beast with faster speeds and a trio of hair-raising loops. The newest addition, the Mælkevejen, ('Milky Way'), zips around the gardens at a lower level.

Aquila

Like the Star Flyer, Aquila (Eagle) is also a nod to the country's most famous astronomer; the ride is named for the constellation that Brahe observed through his 16th-century telescope. The attraction itself is a breathtaking, gut-wrenching swing-and-spinner ride, with centrifugal powers up to 4G that will have you spinning around and upside down at 11m.

Rides for Younger Kids

There's a good choice for younger kids, including a beguiling, sedate twirl through 32 of Hans Christian Andersen's fairy tales at the Flying Trunk. The boat through the Mine allows participants to laser-shoot targets on the way, while there's a vintage car track where young kids can pretend to drive.

★ Top Tips

o Rather than buying single tickets, the unlimited-ride wristband is usually better value.

o In the evening, the lights and lanterns come on and the whole park begins to sparkle.

o Although the free Friday music concerts (summer season only) commence at 10pm, head in by 8pm if it's a big-name act.

o Lockers are available on site.

✖ Take a Break

Tivoli Food Hall (p50) has Hallernes smørrebrød, Thai curry, sushi and local favourite Gorms pizza, and is cheaper than plumping for one of the park's restaurants. It's accessible from outside without a ticket as well.

The Grounds

Beyond the roller coasters, carousels and side stalls is a Tivoli of beautifully landscaped gardens, tranquil nooks and eclectic architecture. Lower the adrenaline under beautiful old chestnut and elm trees and amble around Tivoli Lake, gently rippling with koi carps, goldfish and ducks. Formed out of the old city moat, the lake is a top spot to take a boat out and snap pictures of Tivoli's commanding Chinese Tower, built in 1900.

Illuminations & Fireworks

Throughout summer, Tivoli Lake wows the crowds with its nightly laser and water spectacular. The best spots to catch the show are from the bridge over the lake or the area in front of the Vertigo ride. Another summer-season must is the Saturday-evening fireworks, repeated again from 26 to 30 December for Tivoli's annual Fireworks Festival. For a good view, make a beeline for Plænen (Tivoli's outdoor stage) or the area around the large fountain. For dates and times, see the website.

Live Music

Tivoli delivers a jam-packed program of live music. The indoor Tivolis Koncertsal (Concert Hall) hosts mainly classical music, with the odd musical and big-name pop or rock act. Outdoor stage Plænen is the venue for Fredagsrock, Tivoli's free, hugely popular Friday-evening concerts, which run from mid-April to late September. The acts span numerous

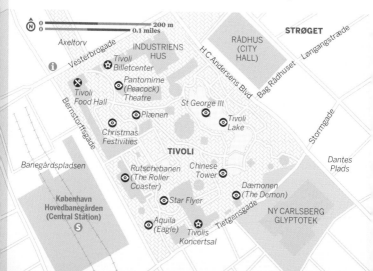

Tivoli's Foodie Pagoda

Since 2021, visitors to Tivoli Gardens have enjoyed the chance to experience some of Denmark's and Europe's most talented chefs at pop-ups at the Japanese Pagoda. The 25m-high pagoda was built in 1900 and is undoubtedly one of the most photographed buildings in Tivoli. Since it opened as a pop-up venue, restaurants such as AOC and Faroese KOKS (both with two Michelin stars), Spanish master-chef Paco Morales (two Michelin stars) and Icelandic Dill (one Michelin star) are some of the restaurants and chefs who have already made their way to the amusement park to serve their unique cuisine to Tivoli's guests. The intention is for the Japanese Pagoda to become a place where you can experience cultures and cuisines from all over the world, with a changing star lineup of chefs.

Mikkel Ustrup, *Senior Director, Nimb @nimbcopenhagen*

genres, from pop, rock and neofolk, to hip-hop, jazz and funk. All tickets are sold at the Tivoli Billetcenter or online through the Tivoli website.

Ballet

Tivoli's brilliant ballet performances take place during summer at the outdoor Pantomime (Peacock) Theatre, with over 300 performances of fairy tales, Hans Christian Andersen stories and modern works. Costumes and sets are often designed by the multitalented Queen Margrethe II of Denmark.

Seasonal Festivities

Even the toughest scrooges find it hard not to melt at the sight of Tivoli in November and December, when the park turns into a Yuletide winter wonderland. The Tivoli Christmas market is one of the city's best-loved traditions, heady with the scent of cookies, pancakes and *gløgg* (mulled wine). It's a good spot to pick up nifty Nordic *nisse* (gnomes) and more. At Halloween, the park opens for two weeks with spooky decorations.

Pantomime Theatre

Tivoli's charming Pantomime Theatre debuted in 1874. It's the work of architect Vilhelm Dahlerup, responsible for many of Copenhagen's most iconic buildings, including the Ny Carlsberg Glyptotek and Statens Museum for Kunst. Dahlerup's historicist style shines bright in his Tivoli creation, a colour-bursting ode to the Far East. While plays in the tradition of Italy's Commedia dell'arte are presented here, there are also other performance styles, including modern ballet.

Top Experience

Learn some Danish History at Nationalmuseet

Housed in a former royal palace, Copenhagen's National Museum immerses visitors in millennia of Danish history. Its hefty hoard includes Denmark's fabled Sun Chariot, the well-preserved Huldremose Woman and Viking artefacts. Beyond these Danish icons is an eclectic mix of foreign acquisitions, and there's a great children's wing.

◎ MAP P48, D4

https://en.natmus.dk

Danish Prehistory

Many of the museum's most spectacular finds are in the Prehistory Collection, located on the ground floor. Among these is a finely crafted 3500-year-old Sun Chariot and the spectacular Gundestrup cauldron (pictured), Europe's oldest example of Iron Age silverwork. Then there's the Huldremose Woman, a well-preserved Iron Age time traveller still wrapped in her cloaks.

Danish Middle Ages & Renaissance

The 1st floor harbours medieval and Renaissance objects from 1050 to 1660. Among them are *aquamaniles* (animal-shaped vessels used in Danish churches for handwashing rituals). The most charming of these is a matching pair, consisting of a young man on horseback and the studiously indifferent woman he is attempting to woo. Both vessels narrowly escaped destruction when spotted on a conveyor belt at a quarry in Vigsø.

Stories of Denmark: 1660–2000

One floor up is the *Stories of Denmark: 1660–2000* exhibition, which traces Denmark's evolution from absolute monarchy to modern nation in three chronological sections: Under the Absolute Monarchy 1660–1848; People and Nation 1848–1915; and Welfare State 1915–2000. Topics include Denmark's string of humiliating wartime defeats, which forced this once powerful, conquering land to reassess its global role.

Ethnographic Treasures

The National Museum's ethnographic collection is one of its lesser-known fortes. Items include an extraordinary child's fur from Canada, fastened with 80 amulets, including fox teeth and a herring gull's foot. Such adornments were believed to ward off evil and lure good fortune.

★ **Top Tips**

o Tickets are valid all day, allowing you to leave the museum and return later if you feel like breaking up your explorations. Free lockers are available.

o The museum has a number of self-guided-tour brochures available for downloading on its website. Among these is a one-hour family tour as well as a children's guide to museum highlights.

✕ **Take a Break**

Skip the average museum restaurant for a classic Danish feast at nearby, canal-side Kanal Caféen (p50).

For a post-museum vino, kick back at Ved Stranden 10 (p71).

Tivoli Area

A
B
C
D

1

Ørsteds Parken

Jamers Plads

Larslejsstræde

Norre Voldgade

Vor Frue Plads

Niels Hemmingsensgade

X 4

Sankt Peders Stræde

Studiestræde

Norregade

Skindergade

Vimmelskaftet

9

Larsbjørnsstræde

2

H C Andersens Blvd

Vester Voldgade

Vestergade

Gammeltorv

Nygade

Knabrostræde

Hyskenstræde

Nytorv

Naboløse

Frederiksberggade (Strøget)

Mikkel Bryggers Gade

Heste-Gåsegade

Kompagnistræde

Snaregade

Slutsholms Kanal Vindebrogade

12 ✪

Lavendelstræde

Rådhuspladsen M

Jernbanegade

3

Rådhuspladsen

Farvergade

Løngangstræde

11 ✪

Frederiksholms Kanal

Axeltorv

7 X Vesterbrogade

Industriens Hus

2 ◉ Rådhus

3 ◉

Stormgade

Nationalmuseet

X 5

8 ⊕

◉ Tivoli Gardens

TIVOLI

Museum of Copenhagen

Dantes Plads

6 X

Ny Kongensgade

Vester Voldgade

4

København Hovedbanegården (Central Station) S

Ny Carlsberg Glyptotek

1 ◉

H C Andersens Blvd

10 ✪

Tietgensgade

Ved Glyptoteket

Bernstorffsgade

5

Hambrosgade

Mitchellsgade

Christians Brygge

6

Sydhavnen

For reviews see
◉	Top Experiences	p42
◉	Sights	p49
X	Eating	p49
⊕	Drinking	p50
✪	Entertainment	p51

N
0 —————— 200 m
0 —————— 0.1 miles

A
B
C
D

Sights

Ny Carlsberg Glyptotek

MUSEUM

1 MAP P48, C4

The Glyptotek houses the collection of Carl Jacobsen, founder of Carlsberg, in a fanciful late-19th-century building centred on a palm- and pond-dotted domed winter garden. The collection is divided into two parts: Northern Europe's largest booty of antiquities, including Egyptian mummies, Roman statuary and Nubian relics, and an elegant collection of 19th-century Danish and French art, with works by Rodin, Van Gogh, Manet, Monet and Gauguin. (www.glyptoteket.com)

Rådhus

HISTORIC BUILDING

2 MAP P48, B3

Completed in 1905, Copenhagen's National Romantic–style city hall is the work of architect Martin Nyrop. To the right of the entrance inside is the curious **Jens Olsen's World Clock**, designed by astro-mechanic Jens Olsen (1872–1945) and built at a cost of one million kroner. Regular tours climb the 300 or so steps to the top of the 105m city-hall **tower**, for fabulous city views. (www.kk.dk)

Museum of Copenhagen

MUSEUM

3 MAP P48, C4

In this historic building are beautifully designed exhibits taking you through 14 key historical sites, including Slotsholmen, City Hall Square and the royal palaces. There is a great miniature model of the city where you can light up famous monuments, and there are films of some of the originators of Christiania. It's extremely absorbing. (www.cphmuseum.kk.dk/en)

Eating

Restaurant Mes

DANISH $$$

4 MAP P48, A1

Owned by chef Mads Rye Magnusson (former chef at Michelin-three-starred Geranium), this whimsical, playful place has a moss feature wall is flooded with light and has contemporary black-moulded chairs and exposed light bulbs. This is high-end cooking at a more

Jens Olsen's World Clock

NINA ALIZADA/SHUTTERSTOCK ©

affordable price point: a five-course menu costs 350 DKK. (www.restaurant-mes.dk)

Tivoli Food Hall

MARKET $$

5 MAP P48, A3

Tivoli's food hall is a sleek building serving up 'fast gourmet' fare. It offers a range of international cuisines as well as Danish eats, including bakeries and a wine bar. Local favourites Gorms pizza and Hallernes smørrebrød are here, as is Michelin-starred Kadeau with its first fast-food venture, BobbaBella. The food hall is a part of Tivoli Gardens amusement park, but can be accessed independently. (www.tivoligardens.com)

Kanal Caféen

DANISH $$

6 MAP P48, D4

Dating from the 19th century, this cosy, nautical old-timer was one of Copenhagen's last 'men-only' pubs. Now more inclusive, it comes with a shaded summertime pontoon right on the canal. Order some Linie Aquavit (*snaps* matured at sea in oak-sherry casks) and the Kanal Platter, a hunger-busting feast of classics such as pickled herring, crumbed plaice, and roast pork with pickled red cabbage. (www.kanalcafeen.dk)

Lagkagehuset

CAFE $

7 MAP P48, A3

This 'layer cake house' is a branch of a Danish bakery chain, enduringly popular for its devotion to reliably good pastries, sandwiches and salads. There's some seating and it's handily located inside Copenhagen's main tourist office and opposite Tivoli's main gate. (Vesterbrogade 4B)

Drinking

Nimb Bar

COCKTAIL BAR

8  MAP P48, A4

There are few more sumptuous settings for a cocktail or afternoon tea than under the sparkling ballroom crystal chandeliers (the originals from 1909), at super-chic Hotel Nimb. It was founded by legendary bartender Angus Winchester. Expensive but glorious. (www.nimb.dk)

Lagkagehuset

ANNA SVETLOVA/SHUTTERSTOCK ©

Living Room
CAFE

9 MAP P48, B2

With exposed brick walls, and mis-matched leather armchairs and sofas, spread over three levels and with a lantern-hung, Moroccan-themed tea room, the aptly titled Living Room is a super-cosy (albeit often busy) spot to settle in with a speciality coffee, tea, homemade smoothie or lemonade. Cocktails and other alcoholic libations are also served late into the evening. (www.thelivingroom.dk)

Entertainment

Tivoli Koncertsal
CONCERT VENUE

10 ⭐ MAP P48, B5

The Tivoli concert hall hosts Danish and international classi-cal and contemporary music art-ists and dance companies. Buy tickets online or at the Tivoli Box Office by the main Tivoli Gardens entrance on Vesterbrogade. (www.tivoligardens.com)

Mojo
BLUES

11 ⭐ MAP P48, C3

This place has plenty of soulful atmosphere, making it a great spot to wallow in the blues and various associated genres, from bluegrass

Take a Break

Many visitors to **Ny Carlsberg Glyptotek** (p49) miss its roof-top terrace, an ideal escape on sunny days. Decked out with chairs for lazy lounging, it offers views of the museum's elegant dome and the spire-studded skyline. The rooftop is not accessible in inclement weather.

and zydeco to soul. There are live acts nightly, followed by DJ-spun tunes. The vibe is warm, convivial and relaxed, and there's draught beer aplenty. (www.mojo.dk)

Grand Teatret
CINEMA

12 ⭐ MAP P48, B3

Just off Strøget, this historic theatre from 1923 screens a range of films from European arthouse productions to mainstream dramas. The on-site cafe serves simple bites like goat's-cheese salad and cake, as well as organic, free-trade coffee and top-notch teas, and wines by the glass.

English-language films are pre-sented with Danish subtitles. (www.grandteatret.dk)

SØREN KIERKEGAARD

Explore

Slotsholmen

Slotsholmen is a spire-spiked island, home to Christianborg Slot, centre of government and royalty. It also has Copenhagen's glorious library, the visual delights of the Thorvaldsens Museum, and just south of Slotsholmen lies the stunning Danish Architecture Centre.

The Short List

○ **Christiansborg Palace (p54)** *Explore lavish interiors, innovative tapestries and original fortress ruins in Denmark's house of power.*

○ **Thorvaldsens Museum (p61)** *Enjoy the picture-perfect tableau of every room devoted to great Danish sculptor Bertel Thorvaldsen.*

○ **Det Kongelige Bibliotek (p61)** *Take in the incredible atrium view at Copenhagen's Royal Library, the water-front 'Black Diamond'.*

○ **Dansk Arkitektur Center (p61)** *Whiz down the slide and explore mind-bending exhibitions, at starchitect Rem Koolhaas' innovative BLOX building.*

Getting There & Around

🚌 Slotsholmen is well serviced by bus, with routes 1A, 2A, 9A, 14, 26, 37 and 66 all crossing the island.

Ⓜ The closest metro station is Gammel Strand, just north of Slotsholmen.

⚓ Commuter ferries stop just beside Det Kongelige Bibliotek.

Slotsholmen Map on p60

Søren Kierkegaard statue, Royal Library Garden (p59) GORAN VRHOVAC/SHUTTERSTOCK ©

Top Experience 📸
Explore Borgen, 'the Castle'

The grey-stone, forboding Christiansborg Palace (Christiansborg Slot) will be familiar to some as the setting for the Danish political drama Borgen ('the Castle', the nickname for Christianborg, Denmark's parliament). This is Denmark's power base, home to the Prime Minister's office and Supreme Court, as well as the monarchy.

◉ MAP P60, B2

www.christiansborg.dk

Royal Reception Rooms

The grandest part of Christiansborg is **De Kongelige Repræsentationslokaler** (www.christiansborg.dk), a series of 18 elegant palace rooms and halls used by the queen to hold royal banquets and entertain heads of state. The memorable Queen's Library has a gilded gallery, chandeliers, a ceiling of circling storks painted by Johannes Larsen, and some of the royal family's centuries-old book collection. The Great Hall is home to Bjørn Nørgaard's colourful wall tapestries depicting 1000 years of Danish history. Look for the Adam-and-Eve–style representation of the queen and her husband in a Danish Garden of Eden.

Fortress Ruins

A walk through the crypt-like bowels of Slotsholmen, known as **Ruinerne under Christiansborg** (www.christiansborg.dk), offers a view of ruins of Slotsholmen's original fortress – built by Bishop Absalon in 1167 – and its successor, Copenhagen Castle. Among these remnants are each building's ring walls, plus a well, a baking oven, sewerage drains and stonework from the castle's Blue Tower. The tower is infamous as the place where Christian IV's daughter, Leonora Christina, was incarcerated for treason from 1663–85.

Royal Stables

Completed in 1740, the two curved, symmetrical wings behind Christiansborg Slot belonged to the original baroque palace, which was mostly destroyed by fire in 1794. The wings still house De Kongelige Stalde (p62) and its museum of antique coaches, uniforms and riding paraphernalia, some of which are still used for royal receptions. Among these is the 19th-century Gold Coach, adorned with 24-karat gold leaf, used once annually, to take the Danish Queen from her residence at Amalienborg to Christianborg Castle at New Year.

★ **Top Tips**

○ If you don't have a Copenhagen Card (which covers this and most other sights in the city) and plan on visiting several of the sights at Christiansborg Slot, opt for the combination ticket, which includes access to the Royal Reception Rooms, the Fortress Ruins, the Royal Stables, as well as the surprisingly interesting Royal Kitchen. The ticket is valid for one month.

✗ **Take a Break**

Book a lunch table at the upmarket restaurant Tårnet (p63), in Christiansborg's Tower, owned by prolific restaurateur Rasmus Bo Bojesen. It has exceptional smørrebrød (open sandwiches) and Danish cheeses, beers and a view of Tivoli.

Christiansborg Slotskirke

Architect CF Hansen's austere, 19th-century neoclassical **church** is the location for royal christenings, weddings and funerals.

In 1992, tragedy struck on the day of the Copenhagen Carnival: a stray firework hit the scaffolding surrounding the church and set the roof ablaze, destroying the dome. With no surviving architectural plans of the dome and roof construction to consult, architectural archaeologists systematically recorded the charred remains before painstakingly reconstructing the chapel.

Miraculously, a remarkable frieze by Bertel Thorvaldsen that rings the ceiling just below the dome survived.

The Tower

The 106m-high **palace tower** (www.ft.dk/taarnet) is the city's tallest. The 44m viewing platform offers sweeping views across the capital and rooftops beyond.

Theatre Museum

Dating from 1767, atmospheric Hofteater (Old Court Theatre) is the royal theatre, with special seating for the monarch.

It has hosted everything from Italian opera to local ballet troupes, one of which had fledgling ballet student Hans Christian Andersen.

Taking its current appearance in 1842, the venue is now the **Teatermuseet** (www.teatermuseet.dk). Wander the stage, boxes and

Christiansborg Palace

Layers of History at Christianborg Slot

Christiansborg Slot is an architectural phoenix. The current palace is the latest in a series of buildings to have graced the site, the first of which were medieval castles, followed by an elegant baroque beauty.

Bishop Absalon's Castle

According to medieval chronicler Saxo Grammaticus, Bishop Absalon of Roskilde built a castle on a small islet in the waters off the small town of Havn. The islet would become Slotsholmen. Erected in 1167, the castle was encircled by a limestone curtain wall – the ruins can still be seen under the current complex. Despite frequent attacks, Absalon's creation stood strong for two centuries until a conflict between Valdemar IV of Denmark and the Hanseatic League saw the latter tear it down in 1369.

Copenhagen Castle

By the end of the 14th century, Copenhagen Castle had a moat and a solid, towered entrance. The castle remained the property of the Bishop of Roskilde until 1417, when Erik of Pomerania seized control, turning it into a royal abode. Nipped and tucked over time – Christian IV added a spire to the entrance tower – the castle was completely rebuilt by Frederik IV, evidently with dubious engineering advice. It began to crack under its own weight, leading to its hasty demolition in the 1730s.

Christiansborg: One, Two, Three

The demolition led to the debut of the first Christiansborg Slot in 1745. Commissioned by Christian VI and designed by architect Elias David Häusser, it went up in flames in 1794, its only surviving remnant the Royal Riding Complex, home to the Royal Stables. Rebuilt in the early 19th century, it became the seat of parliament in 1849 before once more succumbing to fire in 1884. In 1907 the cornerstone for the third Christiansborg Slot was laid by Frederik VIII. Designed by Thorvald Jørgensen and completed in 1928, it's a national affair, its neobaroque facade adorned with granite sourced from across the country.

dressing rooms, and see displays of set models, drawings, costumes and period posters tracing the history of Danish theatre. At the time of going to print, it was due to reopen this year after renovations.

Walking Tour 🥾

A Slotsholmen Saunter

While Slotsholmen may look small on a map, this compact island is Denmark's powerhouse. It's here that politicians debate policy, supreme-court judges set precedents and the Queen plays host with the most. This easy meander will have you crossing Copenhagen's most romantic bridge, scanning the city from its tallest tower and relaxing in a secret library garden.

Walk Facts

Start Marmorbroen; Bus 1A, 2A, 9A, 26, 37 to Stormbroen

Finish Ved Stranded 10; Bus 1A, 2A, 9A, 26, 37 to Christiansborg Slotsplads

Length 2km; 1.5 hours

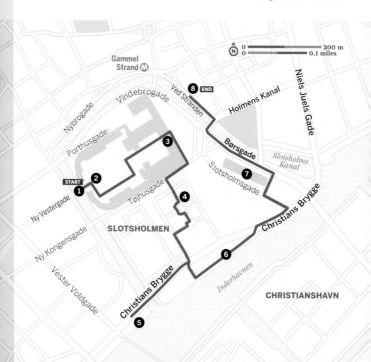

❶ Marmorbroen

Designed by Nicolai Eigtved, the **Marble Bridge** is one of Copenhagen's rococo highlights. Completed in 1745, it dates from the original Christiansborg Slot, which went up in flames in 1794.

❷ Christiansborg Ridebane

The **Riding Ground complex** also survived the fire, offering a glimpse of the palace's original baroque style. The square's only decoration is Vilhelm Bissen's 19th-century equestrian statue of Frederik VII.

❸ Christiansborg Slot Tower

Head through Christiansborg Slot's main entrance to climb the palace tower (p56). Fans of Danish TV drama *Borgen* will know that it's here that Birgitte's mentor Bent Sejrø encourages her to fight for the role of *statsminister*.

❹ Det Kongelige Biblioteks Have

The open archways of the red-brick building facing Christiansborg Slot's south side lead to the secret-feeling **Royal Library Garden**, sitting on Christian IV's old naval port, Tøjhushavnen. Mogens Møller's towering fountain sculpture is an ode to the written word and shoots out water on the hour. Look for the 1918 bronze statue of 19th-century philosopher, poet and theologian Søren Kierkegaard by sculptor Louis Hasselriis.

❺ Dansk Arkitektur Center

This **gallery** (p61) in the Lego-block-esque BLOX south of the *bibliotek* has architecture exhibitions, cafes, a bookshop and a four-storey metallic slide by Carsten Höller.

❻ Det Kongelige Bibliotek

The **library** (p61) connects its Hogwartian reading rooms to its extraordinary extension, the **Black Diamond**. The sleek facade is clad in black granite from Zimbabwe and polished in Italy. It has a cafe, shop and exhibitions. The 6th floor has great views of the gaping atrium and the canal.

❼ Børsen

Head north along the waterfront, then left on to Slotsholmsgade. The old stock exchange, 1625 Børsen (p61), has a narrow, dragon-tailed spire and was once flanked by water on three sides. Its original lead roof was plundered for cannonballs during the 1658–59 Swedish occupation. Today's green-tinged copper roof was added in the 19th century.

❽ Ved Stranden 10

Cross Holmens Bro for a well-earned tipple at this **wine bar** (p71), lined with wine bottles and wooden drawers, that offers canalside seating in summer.

Slotsholmen

Map labels

Snaregade

Knabrostræde

Magstræde

Nybrogade

Stormbro

Slotsholms Kanal

Portugisgade

Bertel Thorvaldsens Plads

1 Thorvaldsens Museum

Christiansborg Ridebane

Christiansborg Slotsplads

Højbro

Vindebrogade

Ved Stranden

Laksegade

Nikolaigade

Admiralgade

Holmens Bro

Holmens Kanal

Havnegade

Havnegade

Niels Juels Gade

Nationalbanken

Christian IV's Bro

8 ✗

Børsen
3 ◉

Børsgade

Slotsholmsgade

Børsgade

Tøjhusgade

Ministerialbygning

Christiansborg Slot ◉

Marmorbroen

De Kongelige Stalde
5 ◉

Tøjhusmuseet
6 ◉

7 ✗

Det Kongelige Bibilioteks Have

Dansk Jodisk Museum **4**

Søren Kierkegaards Plads

Det Kongelige Bibliotek **2** ◉

SLOTSHOLMEN

Christian IV's Bryghus

Prinsensbro

Frederiksholms Kanal

Frederiksholms Kanal

Dansk Arkitektur Center BLOX (150m) ➤

Nv Vestergade

Nationalmuseet

Knippelsbro

CHRISTIANSHAVN

Christians Brygge

Inderhavnen

100 m

N

For reviews see
◉ Top Experiences p54
◉ Sights p61
✗ Eating p63

Sights

Thorvaldsens Museum
MUSEUM

1 ◉ MAP P60, B1

Michael Gottlieb Bindesbøll designed this Greco-Roman–style building, Denmark's first art museum, to house the work of his close friend, superstar Danish sculptor Bertel Thorvaldsen (1770–1844). After four decades in Rome, Thorvaldsen returned to Copenhagen and donated his private collection to the Danish public, and in return the royal family provided this site. The result was this dazzling museum, where Thorvaldsen's bone-white neo-classical sculptures are set against backgrounds of ochre, berry, mustard and royal blue, with zig-zagged and patterned tiles, creating perfect tableaux at every turn. (www.thorvaldsens museum.dk;)

Det Kongelige Bibliotek
LIBRARY

2 ◉ MAP P60, D4

Scandinavia's largest library consists of two very distinct parts: the original 19th-century red-brick building and the head-turning 'Black Diamond' extension, the latter a leaning parallelogram of sleek black granite and smoke-coloured glass. From the soaring, harbour-fronting atrium, an escalator leads up to a 210-sq-metre ceiling mural by celebrated Danish artist Per Kirkeby. Beyond it, at the end of the corridor, is the 'old library' and its Hogwarts-like northern Reading Room, resplendent with vintage desk lamps and classical columns. (www.kb.dk)

Børsen
HISTORIC BUILDING

3 ◉ MAP P60, E2

Not many stock exchanges are topped by a 56m-tall spire formed from the entwined tails of four dragons. Børsen is one. Constructed in the bustling early-17th-century reign of Christian IV, the building is considered one of the finest examples of Dutch Renaissance architecture in Denmark, with richly embellished gables. Its still-functioning chamber of commerce is the oldest in Europe, though the building is closed to the public.

BLOX Architectural Wonder

Located inside architect Rem Koolhaas' harbourside BLOX building, the **Dansk Arkitektur Center** (Map p60, C4; www.dac.dk) hosts interactive changing exhibitions on Danish and international architecture, and features structures to climb inside, virtual reality, and the twisting, chrome Carsten Høller slide. There's also a rooftop cafe with views over the canal and across to the Black Diamond.

Dansk Jødisk Museum
MUSEUM

4 ◉ MAP P60, D4

Step inside the former Royal Boat House, an early-17th-century building once part of Christian IV's harbour complex, and you find an arresting geometric design by Polish-born Daniel Libeskind, which zigzaggingly takes you through Danish Jewish history, as well as telling the story of how over 90% of Danish Jews were evacuated to Sweden over two nights in 1943, with one man's flight vividly documented via a VR headset. (www.jewmus.dk)

De Kongelige Stalde
MUSEUM

5 ◉ MAP P60, B3

Completed in 1740, the two curved, symmetrical wings behind Christiansborg belonged to the original baroque palace, destroyed by fire in 1794. The wings still house the royal stables and its museum of antique coaches, uniforms and riding paraphernalia, some of which are still used for royal receptions. Among these is the 19th-century Gold Coach, adorned with 24-karat gold leaf, used once annually, to take the Danish Queen from her residence at Amalienborg to Christianborg Castle at New Year. (www.kongehuset.dk)

De Kongelige Stald

YELIZAVETA TOMASHEVSKA/SHUTTERSTOCK ©

Tøjhusmuseet MUSEUM

6 MAP P60, C3

The Royal Arsenal Museum has a fearsome collection of canons and medieval armour, pistols, swords and a WWII flying bomb. Even if you're no weapon-phile, you'll find this museum absorbing, with the recreation of a Danish base in Afghanistan and the chance to climb into a PMV hit by a roadside bomb while you hear the choppers above you. Kids can dress up in uniforms. Built by Christian IV in 1600, the 163m-long building is Europe's longest vaulted Renaissance hall. (www.natmus.dk)

Eating

Tårnet DANISH $$

7 MAP P60, C2

Book ahead for lunch at Tårnet, owned by prolific restaurateur Rasmus Bo Bojesen and memorably set inside Christiansborg Slot's commanding tower. Lunch here is better value than dinner, with superlative, contemporary smørrebrød that is among the city's best. While the general guideline is two smørrebrød per person, some of the à la carte versions are quite substantial (especially the tartare), so check before ordering. (www.ft.dk/da/taarnet)

Music at One

If possible, drop into the Black Diamond at **Det Kongelige Bibliotek** (p61) at 1pm, when the usually quiet space breaks into a dramatic, three-minute soundscape, played through a special 12-channel speaker system. Created by Danish composer Jens Vilhelm Pedersen (aka Fuzzy) and titled *Katalog* (Catalogue), the work consists of 52 individual electro-acoustic compositions, one for each week of the year and inspired by some of the library's treasures.

Kayak Bar PUB FOOD $$

8 MAP P60, F3

This laidback bar at the water's edge has rib-sticking dishes such as fish and chips, burgers and mussels. Ideal post-kayak on the canal, it's run by Kayak Republic (p24) and caters to a lively, youthful crowd. It's an inviting setting, especially for a summer sunset. (www.kayakbar.dk/kajak)

Explore ⊕

Strøget & Around

Pedestrianised Strøget (pronounced 'stroll') weaves through Copenhagen's historical heart from Rådhuspladsen to Kongens Nytorv. This area's most interesting sights, restaurants, bars and boutiques lie off the main drag, in or around the old Latin Quarter. Among them is Copenhagen's austere, sculpture-graced cathedral and King Christian IV's 17th-century Round Tower, an observatory with a spiralling walkway.

The Short List

○ **Latin Quarter (p68)** Wander around the berry-and-mustard-hued 17th-century university area, so-named as its students used to speak Latin.

○ **Rundetårn (p68)** Follow in the footsteps of mighty kings and astronomers for breathtaking views of the Danish capital.

○ **Vor Frue Kirke (p68)** Admire Bertel Thorvaldsen's most famous sculptures in a cathedral fit for royal weddings.

○ **Schønnemann (p70)** Tuck into traditional smørrebrød (open-faced sandwiches) at a time-warped, 19th-century favourite.

○ **Hay House (p73)** Restyle your home via some beautiful Danish design.

Getting There & Around

🚌 Most major routes skirt the historic centre. Only route 14 traverses it, connecting Nørreport to Vesterbro via Tivoli.

Ⓜ Kongens Nytorv station is off Strøget's eastern end. To the northwest is Nørreport, for the metro and S-train.

Strøget & Around Map on p66

Rundetårn (p68) BIDSTRUP/GETTY IMAGES ©

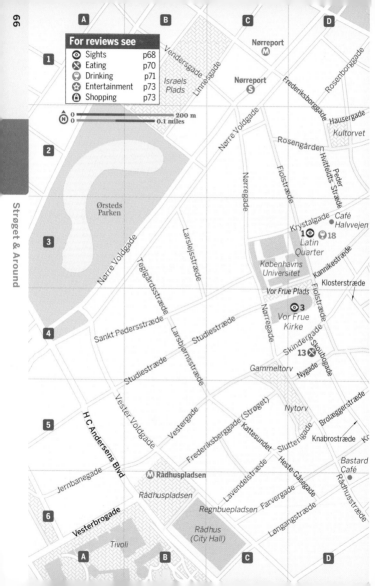

For reviews see

⊙	Sights	p68
❌	Eating	p70
🍷	Drinking	p71
⭐	Entertainment	p73
🔒	Shopping	p73

Strøget & Around

Vendersgade

Nørreport Ⓜ

Linnésgade

Israels Plads

Nørreport Ⓢ

Frederiksborggade

Rosenborggade

Hausergade

Kultorvet

Rosengården

Peder Hvitfeldts Stræde

Nørre Voldgade

Nørregade

Fiolstræde

Ørsteds Parken

Krystalgade

Café Halvvejen

1⊙ 🍷18

Latin Quarter

Nørre Voldgade

Larslejsstræde

Teglgårdsstræde

Københavns Universitet

Kannikestræde

Klosterstræde

Fiolstræde

Vor Frue Plads

⊙3

Vor Frue Kirke

Sankt Pedersstræde

Larsbjørnsstræde

Studiestræde

Nørregade

Skindergade

Skoubogade

13❌

Gammeltorv

Nygade

Studiestræde

Vester Voldgade

Vestergade

Nytorv

Brolæggerstræde

Frederiksberggade (Strøget)

Kattesundet

Slutterigade

Knabrostræde

H C Andersens Blvd

Hestemøllestræde

Bastard Café

Jernbanegade

Ⓜ Rådhuspladsen

Lavendelstræde

Rådhusstræde

Rådhuspladsen

Gåsegade

Farvergade

Regnbuepladsen

Løngangstræde

Vesterbrogade

Rådhus (City Hall)

Tivoli

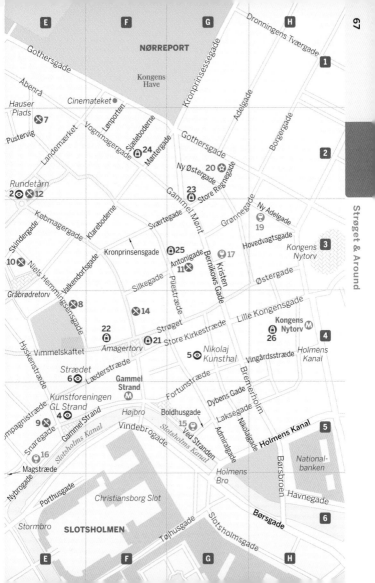

Sights

Latin Quarter AREA

1  MAP P66, D3

Bordered by Nørre Voldgade to the north, Nørregade to the east, Vestergade to the south and Vester Voldgade to the west, the Latin Quarter gets its nickname from the presence of the old campus of **Københavns Universitet** (Copenhagen University), where Latin was once widely spoken. This is one of Copenhagen's most atmospheric districts, dotted with historic, pastel-hued buildings and postcard-pretty nooks. Among the latter is **Gråbrødretorv** (Grey Friars' Sq), which dates from the mid-17th century.

Rundetårn HISTORIC BUILDING

2  MAP P66, E2

The 34.8m-high red-brick 'Round Tower' has an unusual, spiralling slope (rather than steps) to reach the top. King Christian IV built it in 1642 as an observatory (still in use, as Europe's oldest) as well as a tower for the new university church, Trinitatis. You'll also be following in the hoof-steps of Tsar Peter the Great's horse and, according to legend, the track marks of a car that made its way up the tower's spiral ramp in 1902. (www.rundetaarn.dk)

Vor Frue Kirke CATHEDRAL

3  MAP P66, D4

Founded in 1191 and rebuilt three times after devastating fires, Copenhagen's neoclassical cathedral

Gråbrødretorv, Latin Quarter

EQROY/SHUTTERSTOCK ©

dates from 1829. Designed by CF Hansen, its lofty, vaulted interior houses Bertel Thorvaldsen's statues of Christ and the apostles, completed in 1839 and considered his most acclaimed works. In fact, the sculptor's depiction of Christ, with comforting open arms, remains the most popular worldwide model for statues of Jesus. In May 2004, the cathedral hosted the wedding of Crown Prince Frederik to Australian Mary Donaldson. (www.koebenhavnsdomkirke.dk)

Kunstforeningen GL Strand
GALLERY

4 ◉ MAP P66, E5

The HQ of Denmark's artists' union is a good place to catch the cream of contemporary art, with six to eight annual exhibitions of big-name and emerging Danish and international artists, as well as the occasional retrospective. (www.glstrand.dk)

Nikolaj Kunsthal
GALLERY

5 ◉ MAP P66, G4

Built in the 13th century, the church of Sankt Nikolaj houses cutting-edge contemporary art shows such as one of the first exhibitions of NFT ('non-fungible tokens' or digital) works in Europe. The centre also houses a snug, well-regarded Danish restaurant called **Maven**. (www.nikolajkunsthal.dk)

Smart Bikes

Copenhagen's non-profit, good-value bike-share program is called **Bycyklen** (www.bycyklen.dk/en/about-bycyklen). Available 24/7, the electric bikes feature GPS, electric motors, puncture-resistant tyres and locks. The bikes can be accessed from docking stations including at Central Station, Vesterport, Østerport and Dybbølsbro S-train stations. To use, you will first need to create an account. Check the website for docking station locations and real-time bicycle availability at each.

Strædet
STREET

6 ◉ MAP P66, E4

Running parallel to crowded Strøget, Strædet is technically made up of two streets, Kompagnistræde and Læderstræde. They're dotted by ceramic shops and artisanal jewellers. Many of Strædet's medieval and Renaissance-era buildings were destroyed in the great fire of 1795, though some do survive. These include the buildings at numbers 23, 25, 31 and 33, all of which date to the first half of the 1700s.

Board Games & Beer

A godsend on rainy days, hugely popular, supercosy **Bastard Café** (see map p66, D6; www.bastardcafe.dk) is dedicated to board games, which line its rooms like books in a library. Some are free to use, while others incur a small 'rental fee'. While away the hours playing an old favourite or learn the rules of a more obscure option.

Eating

Schønnemann
DANISH $$

 7 MAP P66, E2

A Copenhagen institution, Schønnemann has been lining bellies with smørrebrød and *snaps* (small shot of a strong alcoholic beverage) since 1877. Originally a hit with farmers in town selling their produce, the restaurant's current fan base includes revered chefs like René Redzepi; try the smørrebrød named after him: smoked halibut with creamed cucumber, radishes and chives on caraway bread. (www.restaurantschonnemann.dk)

Gasoline Grill
BURGERS $

8 MAP P66, E4

Damn fine, incredibly juicy burgers made of organic beef and topped with organic cheddar too, if that's what you want, served in a no-frills takeaway, with a shelf along the side to snaffle your food. Don't miss the crispy crinkle-cut chips with truffle salt. (www.gasolinegrill.com)

Marv & Ben
NEW NORDIC $$$

 9 MAP P66, E5

Garlanded by Michelin for its value for money, semi-subterranean, dinner-only 'Marrow & Bone' has bold pink paintings on the walls and a high-concept, creative bent to its New Nordic menu, which you can dabble in a la carte or plump for a four- or six-course tasting menu. Dishes are imaginative and evocative, celebrating Nordic landscapes and moods, with the likes of hot smoked salmon, fermented potato and salsify. (www.marvogben.dk)

Aamanns 1921
DANISH $$$

10 MAP P66, E3

Dapper Danes tuck into the virtuoso smørrebrøds with toppings such as matured herring with blackcurrant, pickled beetroot, and watercress, or new Danish potatoes with bayleaf mayonnaise, pickled onions and watercress, created by chef Adam Aamann from locally sourced ingredients. Lunch is a good bet if you don't want to splash out on the more elaborate dinner menu. Lighting is soft, furniture immaculate Danish design, and it's tucked away on a historic cobbled street. (www.aamanns.dk)

The Market
ASIAN, ITALIAN $$

 11 MAP P66, G3

The Market has two incarnations. The Italian cherry picks elements of regional cuisine and gives them a Scandi twist, with dishes such as cod and potato ravioli with shrimp, courgette, tarragon and tomato. Interiors are classy, with long green banquets and tan leather seating. The Asian version provides a poured-concrete, low-lit, stylish setting for pan-Asian, delicately flavoursome grub. (www.themarketcph.dk)

DØP

HOT DOGS $

12 MAP P66, E2

Danes love a good *pølse* (sausage), and hot-dog vans are ubiquitous across Copenhagen. DØP is the best, with a van right beside Rundetårn (Round Tower). Everything here is organic, from the meat and vegetables to the toppings. Options range from a classic Danish roasted hot dog with all the trimmings, to another served with mash, to a new-school vegan tofu version. (www.døp.dk)

La Glace

BAKERY $

13 MAP P66, D4

Copenhagen's oldest *konditori* (pastry shop) has been compromising waistlines since 1870. Slip into its maze of time-warped rooms and succumb to a slice of the classic *valnøddekage* (walnut cake), a cheeky combo of crushed and caramelised walnuts, whipped cream and mocha glacé, or try historic cakes like Princess Thyra, named after a royal from the time of its founding, a choux pastry filled with custard cream and covered with icing. (www.laglace.dk)

Illum Rooftop

INTERNATIONAL $$

14 MAP P66, F4

This high-end, high-rise food court tops a food hall (Illum Underground), and has a cafe and several restaurants overlooking the rooftops of the historic centre. There's fresh seafood at Skagen, rye bread and pastries at Original Coffee, pizza and pasta at Rossopomodoro, and raw food at Paleo. (https://illum.dk)

Drinking

Ved Stranden 10

WINE BAR

15 MAP P66, G5

Politicians and well-versed oenophiles make a beeline for this canal-side wine bar, its enviable

Danish Comfort Food

Cosy, creaky, wood-panelled **Café Halvvejen** (see map p66, D3; www.cafehalvvejen.dk) channels a fast-fading Copenhagen. The menu is unapologetically hearty, generous and cheap for this part of town, with faithful open sandwiches, *frikadeller* (Danish meatballs) and *pariserbøf* (minced beef steak with egg and onions). The deceptively named *miniplatte* offers a satisfying overview of classic Nordic flavours. Whatever you choose, wash it down with a (very generous) shot of akvavit.

cellar stocked with classic European vintages, biodynamic wines and more obscure drops. With modernist Danish design and friendly, clued-in staff, its string of rooms lend an intimate, civilised air that's perfect for grown-up conversation. Discuss terroir and tannins over vino-friendly nibbles like olives, cheeses and smoked meats. (www.vedstranden10.dk)

Ruby
COCKTAIL BAR

16 MAP P66, E5

With a private members' club vibe, but open to all, these are the kind of elegant 18th-century townhouse interiors where you feel in safe hands. Ruby has no signage, making it clear that this is a place for those in the know, who will be rewarded by suave

mixologists whipping up creative, seasonal libations such as Lady Stardust, with gin, toasted croissant, muscat wine, almond, elderflower and champagne, while a lively crowd spills into a labyrinth of cosy, decadent rooms. (www.rby.dk)

1105
COCKTAIL BAR

17 MAP P66, G3

Head in before 11pm for a bar seat at this dark, luxe lounge. Named for the local postcode, its cocktail repertoire spans both the classic and the revisited, and there's a fine collection of whiskies. It attracts a sophisticated 30- and 40-something crowd who appreciate a finely mixed drink and sumptuous living-room atmosphere. (www.1105.dk)

Terrace seating outside Ved Stranden 10 (p71)

CAROLINE HADAMITZKY/LONELY PLANET ©

Democratic Coffee

COFFEE

18 MAP P66, D3

Students, tourists and locals all flock to Democratic Coffee, where the long wooden coffee bar offers espresso as well as V60-brewed coffee, and the freshly baked croissants are contenders for the city's finest, especially the popular almond ones. (Watch your clothes: the filling is rich and runny.)

Palæ Bar

PUB

19 MAP P66, H3

The air may no longer be thick with tobacco, but the intrigue continues at this unapologetically old-school drinking den. A traditional hit with journalists, writers and politicians, it draws an older local crowd, here to catch up, debate, play chess or tap their fingers to free live jazz, the latter usually offered once a month on Sunday (check the website for dates). (www.palaebar.dk)

Entertainment

Jazzhus Montmartre

JAZZ

20 MAP P66, G2

Since the late 1950s this has been one of Scandinavia's great jazz venues, with past performers including Dexter Gordon, Ben Webster and Kenny Drew. It's undergoing refurbishment, and until reopening, concerts take place at other venues around the city. See the website for details. (www.jazzhusmontmartre.dk)

Cinemateket

Cinephiles flock to the Danish Film Institute's **Cinemateket** (see map p66, F1: www.dfi.dk), which screens around 70 films per month, including twice-monthly classic Danish hits (with English subtitles) on Sundays. The centre also houses an extensive library of film and TV literature, a 'videotheque' with more than 1500 titles – including feature films, shorts, documentaries and TV series – as well as a shop and restaurant-cafe.

Shopping

Hay House

DESIGN

21 MAP P66, F4

Rolf Hay's fabulous interior-design store sells its own coveted line of furniture, textiles and design objects, as well as those of other fresh, innovative Danish designers. Easy-to-pack gifts include anything from notebooks and ceramic cups, to sublimely tasteful building blocks for kids. (www.hay.dk)

Illums Bolighus

DESIGN

22 MAP P66, F4

A wonderland of Danish design, with four floors packed with all things Nordic and beautiful, from Christmas *nisse* (gnomes) to sleek silverware, and from iconic

Danish Design

Visit a Copenhagen home and you'll invariably find Poul Henningsen lamps hanging from the ceiling, Arne Jacobsen or Hans Wegner chairs in the dining room, and the table set with Royal Copenhagen dinner sets, Stelton cutlery and Bodum glassware. Here, good design is not just for museums and institutions: it's an integral part of daily life.

Iconic Chairs

Modern Danish furniture is driven by the principle that design should be tailored to the comfort of the user – a principle most obvious in Denmark's world-famous designer chairs. Among the classics is Hans Wegner's Round Chair (1949). Proclaimed 'the world's most beautiful chair' by US *Interiors* magazine in 1950, it would find fame as the chair used by Nixon and Kennedy in their televised presidential debates in 1960.

The creations of modernist architect Arne Jacobsen are no less iconic. Designed for Copenhagen's Radisson Blu Royal Hotel, the Egg Chair (1958) is the essence of jet-setting mid-century modernity. His revolutionary Ant Chair (1952), the model for stacking chairs found in schools and cafeterias worldwide, found infamy as the chair on which showgirl Christine Keeler (from the British Profumo Affair) sat in a 1960s Lewis Morley photograph.

Switched-on Lighting

Danish design prevails in stylish lamps as well. The country's best-known lamp designer was Poul Henningsen (1894–1967), who emphasised the need for lighting to be soft, for the shade to cast a pleasant shadow and for the light bulb to be blocked from direct view. His PH5 lamp (1958) remains one of the most popular hanging lamps sold in Denmark today.

The popularity of fellow modernist designer Verner Panton is no less enduring. Like Henningsen, Panton was interested in creating lighting that hid the light source, a goal achieved to playful effect with his signature Flowerpot lamp (1968). The designer, who worked for Arne Jacobsen's architectural office from 1950 to 1952, would also go down as an innovative furniture designer, his plastic single-piece Panton Chair (1967) one of the 20th century's most famous furniture pieces.

Danish lighting to sheepskin mittens or soft wool beanies. (www.illumsbolighus.dk)

Storm FASHION & ACCESSORIES

23 🔒 MAP P66, G2

Storm is stacked with trendsetting men's and women's labels such as Haider Ackermann, Kitsuné and Thom Browne. There are Stan Ray, Distressed Fox and Basquiat T-shirts, statement sneakers, boutique fragrances, art and design tomes, fashion magazines and jewellery. (www.stormfashion.dk)

Baum und Pferdgarten FASHION & ACCESSORIES

24 🔒 MAP P66, F2

Designers Rikke Baumgarten and Helle Hestehave are the creative forces behind what is one of Denmark's most respected women's fashion brands. While there's no shortage of pared-back Copenhagen chic, the collections here always fuse a sense of quirkiness, fun and subversiveness. Expect sharp, structured silhouettes, playful prints and beautiful fabrics. (www.baumundpferdgarten.com)

Han Kjøbenhavn FASHION & ACCESSORIES

25 🔒 MAP P66, G3

While we love the uncluttered modernist fit-out, it's what's on the

Monday & Sunday Closures

Many of Copenhagen's museums are closed on Mondays (especially outside the summer season), making Monday the ideal day for a little Danish retail therapy. The worst day to shop is Sunday, when numerous smaller stores are shut.

racks that will hook you: simple, beautifully crafted men's threads that merge Scandinavian sophistication with street smarts and a hint of old-school Danish working-class culture. The label has often collaborated with other designers, like Australian shoemaker Teva and American woolwear veteran Pendleton. In-store accessories include Han's own range of painfully cool eyewear. (www.hankjobenhavn.com)

Magasin du Nord DEPARTMENT STORE

26 🔒 MAP P66, H4

The city's largest (and oldest) department store covers an entire block on the southwestern side of Kongens Nytorv. As well as the global fashion brands are plenty of local labels and design, including Wood Wood, Won Hundred and Baum und Pferdgarten. Head to the basement or top floor for gourmet eats. (www.magasin.dk)

Explore ◈
Nyhavn & the Royal Quarter

Gateway to the sea, 17th-century Nyhavn (pronounced 'new-hown'; meaning 'new harbour') used to be thronged by sailors indulging in R&R at its bars and brothels. Hans Christian Andersen lived here for 18 years in the 1800s. Today, tourists flock here for its jewel-bright townhouses, ship masts, boat trips and foaming ale. Nearby lie the royal palace, Design-museum, the Marble Church and, further north, the Little Mermaid statue.

The Short List

○ **Designmuseum Danmark (p78)** *Salivate over design classics in a rococo ex-hospital.*

○ **Nyhavn (p82)** *Amble along this colour-popping historic harbour.*

○ **Amalienborg Slot (p82)** *Snoop around the Danish royals' downtown digs.*

○ **A Terre (p84)** *Taste playful French-Danish cuisine paired with perfect wines.*

○ **Nebbiolo Antipasti (p86)** *Drink natural wines accompanied by work-of-art snacks.*

Getting There & Around

Ⓜ Kongens Nytor station is 200m southwest (four lines).

🚌 Route 26 serves the centre. Route 66 goes to Slotsholmen and Tivoli. Catch the 350S for Botanisk Have (Botanic Garden) and Nørrebro.

⛴ Harbour buses stop at Nyhavn.

Nyhavn & the Royal Quarter Map on p80

Top Experience 📷

Admire Danish Design at the Designmuseum

Reopening in 2022 following a two-year redesign, Designmuseum Danmark houses a stupendous applied-art collection in a converted 18th-century hospital. It spans everything from the world's finest collection of Japanese samurai tsubas (sword rests) to the mid-century-modern chairs and lamps that still adorn many Danish households. If you're interested in design, you will love this.

◎ MAP P80, D4

www.designmuseum.dk

Contemporary & the Future

Begin your visit via the museum's temporary exhibitions, which address issues such as sustainability, from an organically grown chair to an early electric vehicle.

Fabulous Fabrics

The displays of textiles, fashion and accessories are presented in suspended perspex, as well as some of the museum's original cabinets and drawers. Textiles include ancient fabrics from Peru, a design of cockerels by Picasso, and spirals by Frank Lloyd Wright.

Wonder

The most eccentric objects of the museum's collection are displayed in the series of 'Wonder' rooms. First, you visit the 19th-century ephemera of keen collector Jacob Frohne, followed by snuff boxes and silverware, and a 17m-long display case showing laid-out dining tables, from 1500 to 2013. Another room is devoted to the museum's mesmerising collection of tsubas, Japanese samurai sword rests.

Twentieth-Century Design

The final swathe of displays takes you through a head-spinning array of Danish design classics. It explores the genesis of Danish design, with its roots in simple household furniture, and inspiration from organic forms. There's a firmament of mid-century greats, including Hans Wegner, Børge Mogensen, Finn Juhl, Louis Poulsen and Arne Jacobsen. A pop-art room is packed with wiggly Verner Panton chairs and Alexander Calder mobiles.

★ Top Tip

o The museum shop has beautiful, design-orientated books, unique ceramics, glassware and jewellery, while in the cafe you can enjoy sitting in design-classic chairs while admiring lamps and glass cases by Danish great Kaare Klint.

✗ Take a Break

Head to the museum's beautifully designed **Format** (www.designmuseum.dk/besog-os/cafe) for salads, smørrebrød and sweet treats. In the warmer months, diners can kick back in the museum's historic, leafy courtyard.

If it's dinnertime, savour seasonal dishes, cured meats and quality wines at nearby Pluto (p114).

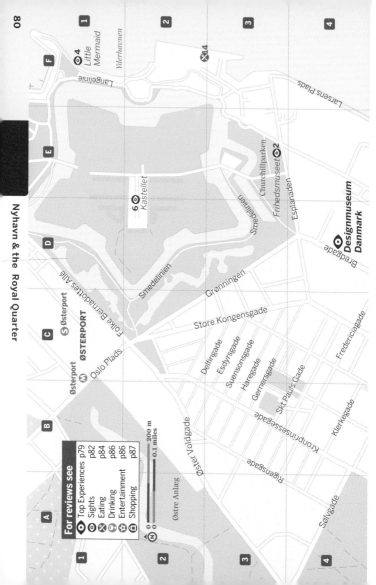

1
2
3
4

A **B** **C** **D** **E** **F**

Little Mermaid ⊙4

Ydernavnen

✕14

Langelinie

Larsens Plads

Kastellet ⊙6

Churchillparken
Frihedsmuseet ⊙2
Smedelinien
Esplanaden

Designmuseum Danmark ⊙
Bredgade

Ø Østerport
ØSTERPORT
Folke Bernadottes Allé

Smedelinien
Grønningen

Store Kongensgade

Østerport
Ⓜ Oslo Plads
ØSTERPORT

Delfingade
Esdyrsgade
Suensonsgade
Haregade
Gernersgade
Skt Pauls Gade
Fredericiagade
Klerkegade

Kronprinsessegade
Rigensgade
Sølvgade

Øster Voldgade

Østre Anlæg

For reviews see
◆ Top Experiences p79
⊙ Sights p82
✕ Eating p84
🍸 Drinking p86
🎭 Entertainment p86
🛍 Shopping p87

0 ————— 200 m
0 ————— 0.1 miles
N

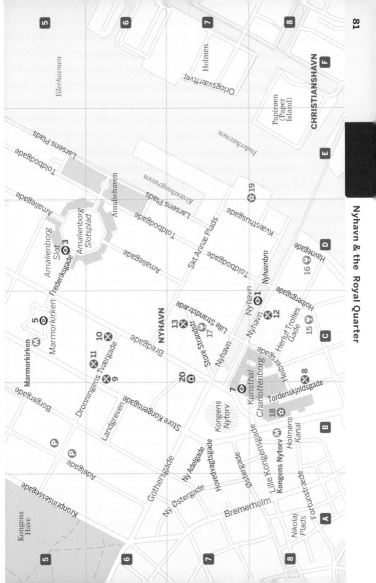

Sights

Nyhavn

CANAL

1 ◎ MAP P80, C8

The 17th-century harbour of Nyhavn is lined by chalky coloured houses that look as if they could illustrate a storybook. Suitably enough, this was a favoured address for Hans Christian Andersen, who lived not only at No 20, where he wrote *The Tinderbox*, *Little Claus and Big Claus* and *The Princess and the Pea*, but also at Nos 18 and 67. The canal was built to connect main square Kongens Nytorv to the harbour and was long a haunt for sailors and writers.

Frihedsmuseet

MUSEUM

2 ◎ MAP P80, E3

After the previous museum was destroyed in an arson attack in 2013, this contemporary space was created to evoke the Danish resistance against their Nazi occupiers from 1940 to 1945. Many of the displays are underground, and you get to try your hand at decoding secret messages, tapping phone calls and even printing an illegal magazine. It's a good one for kids as well as adults. (http://en.natmus.dk)

Amalienborg Slot

PALACE

3 ◎ MAP P80, D5

Home of the current queen, Margrethe II and her descendants, Amalienborg Slot consists of

Royal Guards, Amalienborg Slot

four austere 18th-century palaces around a large cobbled square. It's well worth swinging by to see the changing of the guard, which takes place here daily at noon, the new guard having marched through the city centre from the barracks on Gothersgade at 11.30am. (www. kongernessamling.dk/amalienborg)

The Little Mermaid STATUE

4 MAP P80, F1

In 1909 the Danish beer baron Carl Jacobsen commissioned sculptor Edvard Eriksen to create a statue of the Little Mermaid. Over the years it has suffered several decapitations and lost limbs at the hands of vandals and protesters. Carlsberg thus commissioned Danish artist Bjørn Nørgaard to create a new 'genetically altered' version in 2006, which stands nearby and is perhaps truer in spirit to Hans Christian Andersen's bleak fairy tale.

Marmorkirken CHURCH

5 MAP P80, C5

Consecrated in 1894, the copper-green dome of the Marble Church (officially Frederikskirken) dominates the city skyline. The dome, inspired by St Peter's in Rome, offers superb city views. Despite the name, it's not marble. The church was commissioned by Frederik V, with work beginning in 1749, but spiralling costs saw the project mothballed. Denmark's wealthiest 19th-century financier, CF Tietgen, bankrolled the project's revival, but in limestone. (www.marmorkirken.dk)

Best by Design

Our new exhibitions (p78) offer a wide range of experiences, from designers around the world, working to solve global challenges, to the colourful display of the textile collection, co-curated by the Danish designer, Henrik Vibskov. And a favourite is the Wunderkammer, displaying historical designs in an impressive and colourful 16m-long exhibition case. Of course, there are also the iconic pieces from the 20th century, in an exhibition made in collaboration with Louisiana Museum of Modern Art and Kunsten in Aalborg.

 Nikolina Olsen-Rule, Head of Communications, @designmuseumdanmark

Kastellet FORTRESS

6 MAP P80, D2

The massive star-shaped fortress of Kastellet was originally commissioned by Frederik III in 1662. Today, the 18th-century barracks are still in use, but you can visit various parts of the site, including the historic windmill, and grassy ramparts, which offer sweeping views of the harbour and the city's copper-cloaked domes and spires. (www.forsvaret.dk)

Kunsthal Charlottenborg

MUSEUM

7 ⊙ MAP P80, B7

Fronting Kongens Nytorv, Charlottenborg was built in 1683 as a palace for the royal family. Home to Det Kongelige Kunstakademi (Royal Academy of Fine Arts) since 1754, it houses topical contemporary art from homegrown and international names. Expect anything from site-specific installations and video art to painting and sculpture. (www.kunsthalcharlottenborg.dk)

Eating

A Terre

FRENCH $$$

8 ✖ MAP P80, C8

Tucked in an elegant street behind the Kongelige Theatre, this French restaurant purrs with grown-up chic and serves creations by French-Danish chef Yves Le Lay such as 'One night in Bangkok' (crab, salted tomato, red curry and holy basil) and Galette Forestière (buckwheat pancake, Comté, king trumpets and egg yolk). Le Lay's brother, Kasper Langkilde, is sommelier, offering perfect pairings, with a penchant for Piedmont, Priorat and Burgundy. (www.aterre.dk)

Rebel

DANISH $$$

9 ✖ MAP P80, C6

Small, split-level Rebel dishes out arresting, high-end modern Danish grub. Its esoteric creations are relatively affordable, and it's received a Michelin Bib Gourmand. The setting is minimalist, all the better for concentrating on taste-sensation dishes such as prawn toast with kimchi mayo and beef tartare with pickled red-currant, herbal mayo and mustard cress. Trust the sommelier's wine choices, which include extraordinary Old and New World drops. (www.restaurantrebel.dk)

AOC

NEW NORDIC $$$

10 ✖ MAP P80, C6

In the vaulted cellar of a 17th-century mansion, this intimate, two-starred Michelin standout thrills with evocative, often surprising Nordic flavour combinations, such as gooseberry with Oscietra Caviar, and mackerel with glass cabbage and pumpkin juice. Diners choose from two tasting menus, and reservations should be made around a week in advance, especially for late-week dining. (www.restaurantaoc.dk)

District Tonkin

VIETNAMESE $

11 ✖ MAP P80, C6

With a playful interior channelling the streets of Vietnam, casual, convivial District Tonkin peddles fresh, hearty banh mi (Vietnamese baguettes), stuffed with coriander, fresh chilli and combos like Vietnamese sausage with marinated pork, homemade pâté and BBQ sauce. The menu also includes silky Vietnamese pho (noodle soup) and rich, tomato-based *xíu mai* (pork and mushroom meatballs). (www.district-tonkin.com)

Gorm's
PIZZA $$

12  MAP P80, C8

On the less-busy, 'shadow' side of the Nyhavn canal, rustic, wood-beamed Gorm's is a rare gem on this most touristy strip. The pizza bases here are thin, crispy and made with sourdough. Toppings are high quality, with both Italian imports and local artisanal items (Funen lamb salami, anyone?). Libations include a handful of local craft beers and a longer cast of cocktails, among them a liquorice-spiked espresso martini. (www.wearegorms.dk)

Union Kitchen
CAFE $$

13 MAP P80, C7

Around the corner from touristy Nyhavn is cognoscenti Union Kitchen, which gets very buzzy in the evening. It's just as appealing by day, with excellent break-fast and brunch choices, from waffles, yoghurt and granola to burgers and seasonal salads. In the evening, tuck into sharing plates of succulent homemade meatballs, Asian cucumber salad, and cockle-warming mac and cheese. Pilsner is served in endearing little flagons. (https://www.theunionkitchen.dk/)

Seaside Toldboden
DANISH $$

14 MAP P80, F2

The boat-shaped, pale-green Customs House sits at the water's edge, and this piece of architectural heritage has been turned into a swanky gastronomic complex, with seven different foodie places to choose from, including

Union Kitchen

CAROLINE HADAMITZKY/LONELY PLANET ©

Nyhavn & the Royal Quarter Eating

Patagonia Grill with Argentinian slabs of beef, pan-Asian Dang Dang, and all-tartar Project Raw. There's a bar and an oyster specialist, and the setting and views are fantastic. (www.seasidecph.dk)

Drinking

Nebbiolo Antipasti BAR

15 MAP P80, C8

There's a seriously well-chosen selection of natural wines here, just like at the original Nebbiolo, just across Nyhavn. But here, to accompany them, you can share a 10-course menu of antipasti snacks, such as focaccia with aubergine dip or beef tartare with bread sauce. You know when you just want to eat antipasti, and skip

Mystery Makers

Bring out your inner Detective Sarah Lund with a **Mystery Makers** (www.mysterymakers. dk) interactive mystery hunt. Explore Copenhagen's history through solving riddles and clues, sometimes by lanternlight, in iconic locations – including Kastellet. Players are given fictional identities and a mystery to solve; it's a stimulating, engaging way to explore Copenhagen's backstory. Suitable for adults and kids aged 12 and above, you will need a minimum of four people to form a team.

the main courses altogether? This bar gives you the opportunity.

Den Vandrette WINE BAR

16 MAP P80, D8

This harbourside wine bar is a favoured hangout for noma staff, either in its snug cellar or at alfresco waterside tables on sunny days. It offers natural and biodynamic drops, its short, sharply curated list of wines by the glass often including lesser-known blends like Terret Bourret–Vermentino. The food is as good as the wine. American chef Dave Harrison uses local seasonal produce for complex snacks such as beef tongue with leek dressing and tabasco or Danish hiramasa, sea-buckthorn dressing and chilli popcorn. (www.denvandrette.dk)

Nebbiolo WINE BAR

17 MAP P80, C7

Tucked behind Nyhavn, this smart, contemporary wine bar and shop is thronged by locals, who come for its wines from smaller, inspiring Italian vineyards and its array of accompanying antipasti, spanning delicious cold cuts and crostini. (www.nebbiolo-winebar.com)

Entertainment

Det Kongelige Teater BALLET, OPERA

18 MAP P80, B8

The opulent Gamle Scene (Old Stage) hosts world-class opera

SERGIO DELLE VEDOVE/SHUTTERSTOCK ©

Skuespilhuset, Architects: Lundgaard & Tranberg

and ballet, including productions from the Royal Danish Ballet. The beautiful baroque building is the fourth theatre to occupy the site. Existentialist Søren Kierkegaard used to come to the opera here, while fairy-tale writer Hans Christian Andersen was a fan and member of the Royal Danish Opera Chorus. Book tickets in advance. (www.kglteater.dk)

Skuespilhuset

THEATRE

19 ⭐ MAP P80, E8

Copenhagen's harbourside playhouse is home to the Royal Danish Theatre and a world-class repertoire of homegrown and foreign plays. Productions range from the classics to provocative contemporary works. Tickets often sell out well in advance, so book ahead if you're set on a particular production. English-language tours are available; see the website for details. (www.kglteater.dk)

Shopping

Klassik Moderne Møbelkunst

DESIGN

20 🅰 MAP P80, C7

Close to Kongens Nytorv, Klassik Moderne Møbelkunst is Valhalla for lovers of Danish design, with a trove of classics from greats like Poul Henningsen, Hans J Wegner, Arne Jacobsen, Finn Juhl and Nanna Ditzel. (www.klassik.dk)

Explore ✴

Christianshavn

Christianshavn channels Amsterdam with its snug canals, outdoor cafes and alternative attitude. It was established by Christian IV in the early 17th century as a commercial centre and military buffer for the expanding city. Equally reminiscent of liberal Amsterdam is the area's most famous attraction, hash-scented, live-and-let-live commune Christiania.

The Short List

○ **Christiania (p90)** Let your hair down in an alt-living heartland, where bucolic paths lead to eclectic abodes.

○ **Vor Frelsers Kirke (p97)** Scale a sky-high tower inspired by Italian baroque architect Borromini.

○ **Kadeau (p98)** Book a table at a Michelin-starred powerhouse inspired by the Baltic island Bornholm.

○ **Christianshavns Bådudlejning & Café (p101)** Watch the world float by at a loved canal-side cafe-bar.

○ **Operæn (p101)** Give in to a night of intrigue and passion at the spectacular, harbourfront Opera House.

Getting There & Around

Ⓜ Christianshavn station is on Torvegade, Christianshavn's main thoroughfare.

🚌 Buses 2A, 40 and 350 cross Christianshavn along Torvegade. Routes 2A and 37 reach Tivoli Gardens and Central Station. Route 350S reaches Nørrebro. Bus 9A reaches Christiania and Operæn.

⛴ Harbour buses stop at Operæn. Alternatively, disembark at Nyhavn and cross the Inderhavnsbroen pedestrian bridge to Christianshavn.

Christianshavn Map on p96

Top Experience 📷
Wander Free-Spirited Christiania

*Picturesque Christianshavn is more about
canals, historic streets and leafy ramparts than
sights. One exception is world-famous commune
Christiania, the city's idealistic '1970s child'. It's
an easy walk from Christianshavn metro and
the canal-side location makes it beautiful for a
waterside saunter. The historic, architecturally
unique Vor Freslers Kirke and Christians Kirke
are also in easy walking distance.*

◎ MAP P96, D4

www.christiania.org

The Freestate, So Far

Christiania began as a newspaper prank, urging the hippie revolutionists to take over an abandoned military camp. Bowing to public pressure, the government allowed the squatters to continue as a social experiment.

Self-governing, ecology-oriented and generally tolerant, Christiania residents did, in time, find it necessary to modify their 'anything goes' approach. A new policy was established that outlawed hard drugs, and the heroin and cocaine pushers were expelled.

Today, the remaining native settlers are very, very old hippies The houses they constructed were often without building permits, on land owned by the public. So, who decides the future of this prime land? In 2022, the Christiania community – descendants of the early settlers, some 700 adults and 150 children – agreed to allow the government to build affordable housing within its parameters. In exchange, the community will receive a favourable government loan to become a legal owner of the northern Vold quarter.

Dyssen

Dyssen is Christiania's best-kept secret. This long, pencil-thin rampart on the eastern side of the old city moat is connected to Christiania's eastern edge by bridge. Running north–south along the rampart is a 2km-long path, studded with beautiful maples and ash, hawthorn, elder and wild cherry trees, not to mention the homes of some rather fortunate Christianites. It's a perfect spot for lazy ambling, slow bike rides or some quiet downtime by the water among the swans, herons, moorhens and coots.

★ **Top Tips**

o From late June to the end of August, 60- to 90-minute guided tours run daily at 3pm. Tours commence just inside Christiania's main entrance on Prinsessegade.

o While taking photos in Christiania is generally fine, don't snap pictures on or around the main drag of Pusher St. The area is lined with illegal cannabis dealers who can become nervous or aggressive if photographed.

o Cannabis is illegal in Denmark and police routinely search people by the exits.

✖ **Take a Break**

For affordable vegetarian grub in a pretty garden, make a beeline for Morgenstedet (p98) in the heart of Christiania. Cash only.

For a more upmarket dinner, reserve a table at Michelin-starred, modern-Danish hotspot Barr (p98), 650m north of Christiania.

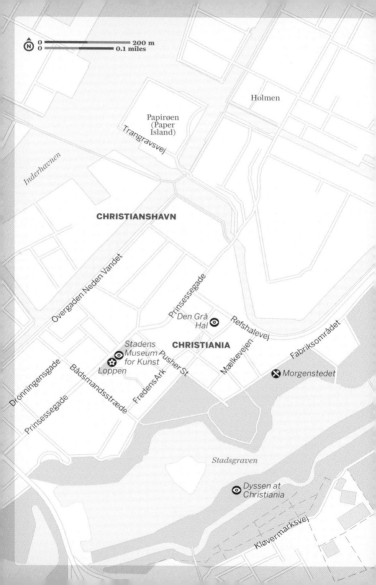

Galloperiet, Stadens Museum for Kunst

Christianites refer to Christiania as 'Staden' (The Town), and the name of art gallery Stadens Museum for Kunst is a tongue-in-cheek play on the more 'establishment' Statens Museum for Kunst. You'll find the place on the 2nd floor of the Loppen building, just beside Christiania's main entrance on Prinsessegade, open from 2pm most days. Head up for rotating exhibitions of contemporary art, spanning both local and international artists, and covering anything from drawings and paintings to installations.

Den Grå Hal

The Grey Hall is the commune's largest cultural venue, able to pack in around 1500 people. It was built in 1893, originally as a riding hall for the military. With the establishment of Freetown Christiania, the space found new purpose as a hub for art and music. Some of the biggest names in music have rocked its weathered walls over the years, among them Bob Dylan, Metallica and Manic Street Preachers. While its calendar is hardly jam-packed these days, the building is worth a look for its architecture and colourful graffiti. In December Den Grå Hal becomes the focal point for Christiania's Christmas festivities, which include a Yuletide market.

Loppen

Its motto might be 'Going out of business since 1973', but 40-something Loppen just keeps on rocking in a former artillery warehouse dating from 1863. The joint started off by spotlighting the local underground scene before evolving into a more prolific music hub. These days, its programme includes an eclectic mix of both local and international talent, from emerging acts to more established names. Indeed, past guests have included top-tier acts like Smashing Pumpkins and Animal Collective.

Walking Tour 🥾

Rustic Refshaleøen

*Houses made of Maersk shipping containers.
Restaurants serving 'holistic cuisine'. Beers
brewed with toasted birch. At Refshaleøen, Danish
avant-garde meets hygge. Walking around, from
one rustic place to the next, it is incredible to think
this dynamic and colourful neighbourhood was
until recently just a dwindling, grey shipyard.*

Walk Facts

Start Copenhill

Finish Reffen

Length 2km; two hours

Harbour buses dock at
Refshaleøen. Bus route 2A
stops at Lynetten between
Copenhill and the Reffen.

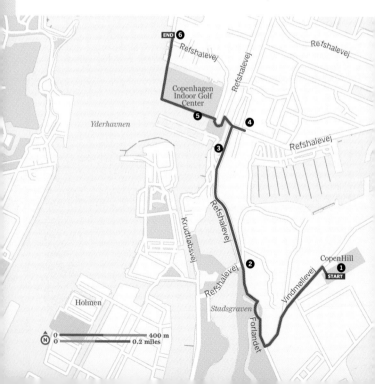

❶ Copenhill

From the heart of Christiania, the 30-minute walk to **Copenhill** (www.copenhill.dk) is green and lovely. The icon of modern Copenhagen is a functioning waste-burning plant, its steaming chimney visible from afar. But come closer to blow off steam yourself; the architectural phenomena has a 450m green-roof ski slope and the world's tallest climbing wall at 85m. Guests can rent skis, but most take the long walk up to the rooftop bar. Take the elevator down to see inside the energy source for 90,000 households.

❷ Vandflyverhangaren

Head towards the sea on Refshalevej where the Danish Navy used to make aeroplanes inside the **Seaplane Hangar**, redesigned as a workshop for the Royal Danish Academy of Fine Arts.

❸ La Banchina

Refshaleøen has many invitations for a swim – here is the first: a lively **cafe** (www.labanchina.dk) with a waterfront patio. Order at the bar and, if you will, follow the slogan: 'Eat. Dip. Repeat.' Winter visitors will enjoy the sauna, but book ahead.

❹ Lille Bakery

For gourmand visitors, **Lille Bakery** (www.lillegrocery.com) alone is worth a trip to the Refshaleøen. Since opening in 2018, the low-key loft establishment has enjoyed a reputation for quality food at competitive prices.

❺ Urban Rigger

Lauded architecture firm BIG appears to enjoy Lego. **Urban Rigger** (www.urbanrigger.dk) is a housing complex made of stacked Maersk shipping containers standing on a harbour quay; each has two student apartments with a shared bathroom and kitchen. Closer to the Reffen, the CPH Village is another block of tiny homes made from containers.

❻ Reffen

Reffen (https://reffen.dk) is one of the best spots to dine, drink and chill on a warm summer evening. The harbourside street-food market is a veritable village of converted shipping containers, peddling sustainable bites from across the globe. Options include the Gambian Baobab, Filipino BBQ and a Danish hot dog serving the best of remoulade. .

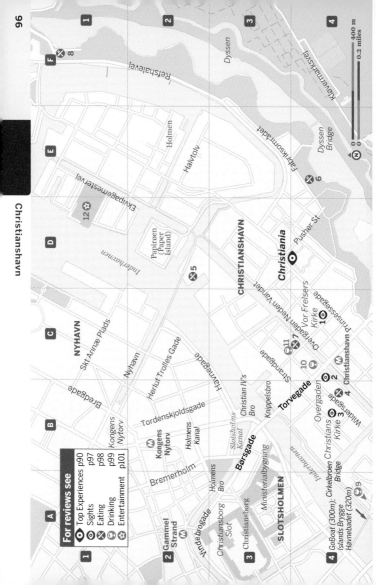

Sights

Vor Frelsers Kirke   CHURCH

1 🎯 MAP P96, C4

It's hard to miss this 17th-century church and its 95m-high spiral tower. For a soul-stirring city view, make the head-spinning 398-step ascent to the top – the last 150 steps run along the outside rim of the tower, narrowing to the point where they literally disappear at the top. Inspired by Borromini's tower of St Ivo in Rome, the spire was added in 1752 by Lauritz de Thurah. Inside the church, highlights include an ornate baroque altar and elaborately carved pipe organ from 1698.

For crowd control, tickets are only sold online. But the receptionist sells water! (www.vorfrelserskirke.dk)

Overgaden   GALLERY

2 🎯 MAP P96, C4

Rarely visited by tourists, this nonprofit art gallery runs about 10 exhibitions annually, putting the spotlight on contemporary installation art and photography, usually by younger artists, both Danish and international. The gallery also runs a busy calendar of artist talks, lectures, performances, concerts and film screenings. See the website for upcoming events. (www.overgaden.org)

Vor Frelsers Kirke

Islands Brygge Havnebadet

Come summer, sun-seeking locals gravitate to **Islands Brygge Havnebadet** (https://svoemkbh.kk.dk/indhold/havnebade), central Copenhagen's most popular outdoor baths. Located just south of Christianshavn in Islands Brygge, its trio of pools sit right in Copenhagen's inner harbour. Water quality is rigorously monitored and the lawns, BBQ facilities and eateries make it a top spot to see and be seen on a warm summer day, whether you get wet or not.

Christians Kirke   CHURCH

3 MAP P96, B4

Named in honour of Christian IV – who founded Christianshavn in the early 17th century – Christians Kirke is well known for its unusual rococo interior. This includes tiered viewing galleries more reminiscent of a theatre than a place of worship. The church was built between 1754 and 1759, serving Christianshavn's sizeable German congregation until the end of the 19th century. (www.christianskirke.dk)

Eating

Kadeau   NEW NORDIC $$$

4 MAP P96, B4

The big-city spin-off of the Bornholm original, this Michelin-two-starred standout has firmly established itself as one of Scandinavia's gastronomic powerhouses. Whether it's salted and burnt scallops drizzled with clam bouillon, or an unexpected combination of lardo, thyme, cherry blossom and Korean pine, each dish manages to evoke moods and landscapes with extraordinary creativity and skill.

The wine list is a thrilling, enlightening showcase of smaller producers and natural drops, and service is warm, genuine and knowledgeable. Book ahead. (www.kadeau.dk)

Barr   SCANDINAVIAN $$$

5 MAP P96, D2

Meaning 'barley' in old Norse, oak-lined Barr offers polished, produce-driven takes on old North Sea traditions. The small plates are a little hit and miss, with standouts including sourdough pancakes with caviar. You'll need about four small plates per person; a better-value option is to savour the pancakes and fill up on the fantastic schnitzel or *frikadeller* (Danish meatballs). (www.restaurantbarr.com)

Morgenstedet   VEGETARIAN $

6 MAP P96, E4

A homey, hippy bolthole in the heart of Christiania, Morgenstedet offers a short, simple blackboard menu. There's usually one soup, plus two or three mains with a choice of side salads. Whether it's cauliflower soup with chickpeas and herbs or creamy potato gratin, options are always vegetarian, organic and delicious, not to mention best devoured in the blissful cafe garden. Cash only.

Cafe Wilder
DANISH $$

7 MAP P96, C4

With its crisp white linen and circular sidewalk tables, this corner classic feels like a Parisian neighbourhood bistro. It's actually one of Copenhagen's oldest cafes, featured several times in the cult TV series *Borgen*. Relive your favourite scenes over beautiful lunchtime smørrebrød (open sandwiches) or Franco-Danish dinner mains like tender Danish pork with sweet-potato croquette and a black-currant sauce. (www.cafewilder.dk)

noma
NEW NORDIC $$$

8 MAP P96, F1

In culinary history the ground-breaking noma is the synonym for 'New Nordic', a movement known today for purity, simplicity and freshness. Since foundation in 2003, noma has not only grown in influence: the restaurant now occupies an entire urban farm where everything from tableware to vinegars are made from scratch. The menu is seasonal, following the three themes of ocean, vegetables and forest. Reservations are essential.

Book online on designated dates approximately three months in advance of the start of each booking period. Tables can be booked for two, four, six or eight guests, and must be prepaid. (www.noma.dk)

GoBoat

The **GoBoat** (www.goboat.dk) kiosk beside Islands Brygge Havnebadet rents out small solar-powered boats that let you explore Copenhagen's harbour and canals independently. Most people go for two hours (900kr), enough time to sail around the canals of the Danish Parliament. You don't need prior sailing experience and each comes with a built-in picnic table. (Get supplies at the superb **Andersen Bakery** around the corner.) Boats seat up to eight and rates are per boat, so the more in your group, the cheaper per person.

Drinking

ROAST Coffee
COFFEE

9 MAP P96, A4

This top-of-the-line micro roaster has a small front serving the freshest of grind nearby the baths at Islands Brygge. Watching the barista measure grams and millilitres to brew the 'pour over' is like observing a science project. It tastes of good ethics, too; the company pays coffee farmers 50% of the retail price, a trade deal going beyond Fair Trade and other programmes. (www.roast.com)

The Danish Table

Not only is Copenhagen home to 23 Michelin stars, it's also the stomping ground of an ever-expanding league of bold, brilliant young chefs turning top produce into groundbreaking innovations and putting new verve into long-loved classics. So grab a (beautifully designed) fork and find a spot at the coveted Danish table.

Beyond New Nordic

While the New Nordic cuisine served at hotspot restaurants like Michelin-starred **Kadeau** (p98) continues to thrill food critics, bloggers and general gluttons, Copenhagen's food scene continues to evolve. Numerous chefs from high-end kitchens have since opened their own restaurants, among them Marchal, **Restaurant Mes** (p49) and Kokkeriet. Most of these offer simpler, more affordable food but don't skimp on quality and innovation: a 'democratisation' of the gourmet dining experience. Many are also taking a less dogmatic approach to contemporary Nordic cooking, using the odd non-regional influence or spice without fear of Nordic culinary damnation. A noma alumnus is behind hugely popular taquería **Hija de Sanchez** (p136), one of a growing number of casual, high-quality international dining spots that also includes **Slurp Ramen Joint** (p114).

Danish Classics

Despite the New Nordic revolution, old-school Danish fare remains a major player on the city's tables. Indeed, tucking into classics such as *frikadeller* (meatballs), *sild* (pickled herring) and Denmark's most famous culinary export, smørrebrød (open sandwiches), at institutions such as **Schønnemann** (p70) is an integral part of the Copenhagen experience. The basic smørrebrød is a slice of bread topped with any number of ingredients, from roast beef or pork to juicy shrimps, pickled herring, liver pâté or fried fish fillet. The garnishes are equally variable, with the sculptured final product often looking too good to eat. In the laws of Danish smørrebrød, smoked salmon is served on white bread, and herring on rye bread. Whatever the combination, the iconic dish is best paired with akvavit and an invigorating beer.

Cafe Wilder (p99) with Eiffel Bar in the background

Christianshavns Bådudlejning & Café BAR

10 MAP P96, C4

Right on Christianshavn's main canal, this festive, wood-decked cafe-bar is a wonderful spot for drinks by the water. It's a cosy, affable hangout, with jovial crowds and strung lights. There's grub for the peckish and gas heaters and tarpaulins to ward off any northern chill. (www.baadudlejningen.dk)

Eiffel Bar BAR

11 MAP P96, C3

Don't be fooled by the name: dark, wood-panelled Eiffel Bar is a red-blooded Danish dive bar, and all the better for it. The joint dates from 1737, when it was a hit with local sailors. The beer is cheap, with all the standard local brews on tap, plus a few Danish craft ales. A solid choice for an animated, amiable, old-school vibe. (www.eiffelbar.dk)

Entertainment

Operæn OPERA

12 MAP P96, D1

Designed by the late Henning Larsen, Copenhagen's state-of-the-art opera house has two stages: the Main Stage and the smaller, more experimental Takkeløftet. The repertoire runs the gamut from blockbuster classics to contemporary opera. While the occasional opera is sung in English, all supertitles are in Danish only. Tickets can be booked directly via the website. (www.kglteater.dk)

Explore

Nørreport

Nørreport and its surrounds blend market stalls, restaurants and bars with distinguished art collections. You'll find appetite-piquing Torvehallerne KBH and the quietly hip strip of Nansensgade, dotted with atmospheric eating and drinking spots. The area is also home to several flagship sights, among them Denmark's National Gallery and Rosenborg Slot. The latter skirts manicured Kongens Have.

The Short List

○ **Rosenborg Slot (p104)** Lust after the Danish crown jewels at a Renaissance castle fit for a fairy tale.

○ **Statens Museum for Kunst (p108)** Rub proverbial shoulders with homegrown and international masters at Denmark's progressive national art museum.

○ **Torvehallerne KBH (p110)** Graze, swill and stock the larder with artisanal edibles at Copenhagen's gourmet food market.

○ **Davids Samling (p113)** Envy an exquisite collection of fine and applied art in the former home of a formidable collector.

○ **Høst (p114)** Dine like a top-end epicurean at digestible, kronor-conscious prices.

Getting There & Around

Ⓜ Nørreport station is right beside Torvehallerne KBH.

🚌 Routes 5C and 350S reach Nørrebro. Bus 14 runs through central Copenhagen and is handy for Slotsholmen. Route 6A reaches Vesterbo and Frederiksberg.

Nørreport Map on p112

Torvehallerne KBH (p110) TMA HARDING/SHUTTERSTOCK ©

Top Experience 📷
Visit Christian IV's Renaissance Castle

Moated **Rosenborg Slot** *heaves with blue-blooded portraits and tapestries, royal hand-me-downs and the nation's crown jewels. Built between 1606 and 1633 by Christian IV to serve as his summer home, the Danish royals opened the castle as a museum in the 1830s, while still using it as as their own giant jewellery box. It serves both functions to this day.*

◉ MAP P112, D3

www.kongernessamling.dk/en/rosenborg

Christian IV's Winter Room

Room 1 is the original building's best-preserved room. The rich wooden panelling – adorned with inlaid Dutch paintings – was begun by Court cabinetmaker Gregor Greuss and completed in 1620. Adorning the ceiling are mythological paintings by Danish-born Dutch painter Pieter Isaacsz, the works replacing the room's original stucco ceiling c 1770. Among the room's items is a 17th-century Florentine tabletop, made of inlaid semiprecious stones. Equally fascinating is the Astronomical Clock, which comes with moving figures and musical works. Dating to 1594, the timepiece was made by the renowned Swiss clockmaker Isaac Habrecht.

Christian IV's Bedroom

It's in Room 3 that Denmark's famous 'Builder King', Christian IV, died on 28 February 1648, and it's here that you'll find his nightcap and slippers, as well as the bloodstained clothes from his naval battle of Kolberger Heide in July 1644. The walls, doors and stucco ceiling all date back to Christian IV's time, as does the stucco ceiling in the adjoining toilet. The toilet's fetching blue and white wall tiles date to Frederik IV's refurbishment of the castle in 1705. Some of the tiles are the Dutch original, while others were made in Copenhagen in 1736. Back in the day, a water cistern was used for flushing, with the king's business expelled straight into the moat.

Mirror Cabinet

It mightn't be the 1st floor's most lavish room, but the Mirror Cabinet is certainly its most curious. Inspired by France's Palace of Versailles, the room's mirrored ceiling, floor and walls could sit comfortably on the pages of a 1970s interior design magazine. In reality, the interior is pure baroque, dating to the beginning of the

★ **Top Tips**

∘ To avoid the queues – which can be dishearteningly long in summer – buy your ticket online. It can be sent directly to your phone so there's no need to print it. Buying online also ensures entry in your desired time slot. If you have a Copenhagen Card, however, you will need to get your tickets in person at the castle ticket office.

✕ **Take a Break**

On the other side of Kongens Have, **Lille Petra** (www.andtradition.com) is a quiet and hidden courtyard cafe with sandwiches, soup and ice cream. Look for its petite sign outside a metal door on Kronprinsessegade 4 and give the gate a firm push.

For something upscale, book a table at genteel **Orangeriet** (www.restaurant-orangeriet.dk), in the park's former observatory.

18th century and specially designed for Frederik IV. All the rage at the time, mirror cabinets were commonly featured in the innermost sanctum of a king's suite, usually in connection with the royal bedchamber. Frederik IV's bedchamber was downstairs in Room 4, connected to the Mirror Cabinet by a spiral staircase. If the thought of all these mirrors seems a little kinky, bear in mind that the adjoining room is where the king kept his collection of erotica.

Knights' Hall

Originally a ballroom, the Knights' Hall was completed in 1624 and was the last of the castle's rooms to be furnished. Gracing the walls are the Rosenborg Tapestries, 12 woven works depicting the battles between Denmark and Sweden during the Scanian War (1675–79). The tapestries were a PR exercise of sorts, commissioned by Christian V to flaunt his military prowess. The Knights' Hall is also home to the coronation thrones and a stucco ceiling with four paintings by Hendrick Krock that represent the four regalia: crown, orb, sword and sceptre. Two small chambers run off the hall, one displaying Venetian glassware, the other home to Royal Copenhagen Porcelain's original Flora Danica set, decorated with exquisite botanical motifs.

Basement Cellar Rooms & Green Room

Rosenborg Slot's undisputed pièce de résistance is its basement, home to an extraordinary collection of

Kongens Have

royal regalia and gifts. Some of the dusty bottles in the castle cellar date to the 18th century. The wine is still used on special royal occasions, though it's now merely splashed into more palatable drops as a ceremonial gesture. The northernmost cellar room contains some rather unusual decorative objects, including an 18th-century chandelier made of amber by Lorenz Spengler. At the southern end of the basement is the Green Room, itself laden with intriguing royal paraphernalia. Keep an eye out for Christian IV's riding trappings, used at his coronation in 1596.

Treasury

Just off the Green Room, the Treasury is where you'll find the castle's most valuable treasures. These include Christian IV's spectacular crown, created especially for his coronation by Dirich Fyring in Odense. Made of gold, pearls and table-cut stones and weighing 2.89kg, its features include the figure of a self-pecking pelican feeding its offspring blood (a symbolic representation of the need for rulers to willingly sacrifice their own blood for their subjects). Other showstoppers include the jewel-studded sword of Christian III (crafted in 1551) and the obsessively detailed Oldenburg Horn. Made of silver in the mid-15th century, the horn is believed to have been a gift from Christian I to Cologne's cathedral. It found itself in Danish hands once more after the Reformation.

Kongens Have

Fronting Rosenborg Slot is much-loved Kongens Have (King's Garden). The city's oldest park, it was laid out in the early 17th century by Christian IV, who used it as his vegetable patch. These days it has a little more to offer, including wonderfully romantic paths, a fragrant rose garden and some of the longest mixed borders in northern Europe. It's also home to a marionette theatre, with free performances from mid-July to mid-August (2pm and 3pm Tuesday to Sunday). Located on the northeastern side of the park, the theatre occupies one of the neoclassical pavilions designed by 18th-century Danish architect Peter Meyn.

Top Experience 📷

Explore Denmark's Top-Tier Art Museum

*The **Statens Museum for Kunst** (National Gallery) is Denmark's pre-eminent art institution, its works span centuries of creative expression, from Mategna to Matisse and beyond. Top billing goes to homegrown heavyweights: Golden Age icons Christoffer Wilhelm Eckersberg and Christen Købke, 20th-century mavericks Asger Jorn and Per Kirkeby, and innovators Elmgreen & Dragset.*

◎ MAP P112, D1

www.smk.dk

European Art: 1300–1800

Originally a royal collection, this is where you'll find the museum's Old Masters. These include Rubens' blockbuster *Judgement of Solomon* (c 1617). Look out for a series of paintings by 17th-century Flemish artist Cornelis Norbertus Gijsbrechts: trompe l'œils with an astoundingly modern sensibility. Standout Italian works include Andrea Mantegna's *Christ as the Suffering Redeemer* (c 1495–1500).

Danish & Nordic Art: 1750–1900

Don't miss the quiet rage of Nicolai Abildgaard's *Wounded Philoctetes* (1775) and Johan Christian Dahl's *Winter Landscape near Vordingborg, Denmark* (1829). CW Eckersberg's most celebrated work is *A View through Three Arches of the Third Storey of the Colosseum* (1815–16). What appears to be a faithful panorama of Rome is actually pieced together from three different perspectives.

French Art: 1900–30

SMK's French collection includes an impressive number of works by Henri Matisse. The most famous of these is *Portrait of Madame Matisse* (1905). Also known as *The Green Line*, it's widely considered a masterpiece of modern portrait painting. Other standouts here include André Derain's *Woman in a Chemise* (1906) – a highlight from the artist's Fauvist period.

Modern Danish & International Art

The collection's modern Danish works are especially notable, among them expressionist Jens Søndergaard's brooding *Stormy Sea* (1954) and CoBrA artists such as Asger Jorn. Look out for Bjørn Nørgaard's *The Horse Sacrifice* and *Objects from the Horse Sacrifice,* which document the artist's ritualistic sacrifice of a horse in 1970 to protest the Vietnam War.

★ Top Tips

○ House artists guide free workshops for children on weekends. Working with memories and imagination, easels and brushes, glue pistols and maybe some sticky fingers, the young artists learn about seasonal hues and complementary colours.

○ The museum hosts numerous special events throughout the year, including SMK Fridays. Held around seven times annually (in spring and autumn), it sees the museum open late with art talks, DJs, performances and food. Check details online.

✕ Take a Break

Just 450m east of the National Gallery, **Aamanns Deli & Takeaway** (www.aamanns.dk) serves some of the best smørrebrød in the city.

Nørreport Explore Denmark's Top-Tier Art Museum

Stroll the Torvehallerne Food Market

A mouthwatering ode to the fresh, the tasty and the slow, food market **Torvehallerne KBH** (www.torvehallernekbh.dk) *peddles everything from seasonal herbs and berries, to smoked meats, seafood and cheeses, smørrebrød, fresh pasta and hand-brewed coffee. Spend an hour exploring its glass halls, chatting to vendors, stocking the larder and noshing on freshly cooked meals.*

Walk Facts

⊙ MAP P112, B3

Start Hall 1

Finish Hall 2

Length 200m; 1 hour

M Nørreport

S Nørreport

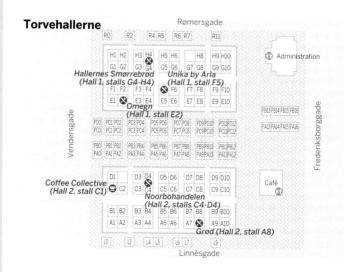

❶ Hallernes Smørrebrød

At well-priced **Hallernes Smørre-brød** (www.hallernes.dk; Stall G4-H4, Hall 1), get scrumptious smørrebrød (get one if you're peckish, two if you're hungry), beers and *snaps* (small shot of a strong alcoholic beverage). Grab a spot at the wooden bar, order a Mikkeller beer and tuck into beautifully presented classics like *fiskefilet* (fish fillet) with remoulade.

❷ Unika

Arla is one of Denmark's mega dairy companies, and **Unika by Arla** (www.arlaunika.dk; Stall F5, Hall 1) is its boutique offshoot. It works with small dairies, artisan cheese-makers and top chefs to produce Nordic-inspired cheeses. Try unpasteurised Kry, considered superior in flavour to pasteurised cheeses. Equally unique are the apple-based dessert wines from Jutland's Cold Hand Winery.

❸ Omegn

Nordic deli **Omegn** (Stall E2, Hall 1) stocks top products from small-scale Danish farms and food artisans. Good buys include Thybo, a sharp cow's-milk cheese from northern Jutland, and handcrafted Borghgedal beer from Vejle. Peckish punters can nibble on cheese and charcuterie, or go old-school with warming *skipperlabskov* (beef stew).

❹ Grød

Holistic **Grød** (http://groed.com; Stall A8, Hall 2) turns stodge sexy with its modern take on porridge. Made-from-scratch options include porridge with gooseberry compote, liquorice sugar, *skyr* (yoghurt) and hazelnuts, or healthier-than-thou grain porridge in carrot juice, served with apple, roasted flaxseeds, raisins and a zingy ginger syrup. Later on, try the chicken congee.

❺ Noorbohandelen

It's never too early for a *skål* (cheers!) at **Noorbohandelen** (Stall C4-D4, Hall 2), stocked with limited-edition and small-batch craft spirits to sample and buy. Options include its own brand of *snaps* and bitters, infused with herbs from the Danish island Møn. The beautiful, customised bottles will remind you of your Scandi sojourn long after the last pour.

❻ Coffee Collective

Save your caffeine fix for **Coffee Collective** (www.coffeecollective.dk; Stall C1, Hall 2), with beans sourced ethically and directly from farmers. It has two espresso blends: one full-bodied and traditional, the other more stringent and Third Wave. If espresso is too passé, order a hand-brewed cup from the Kalita Wave dripper.

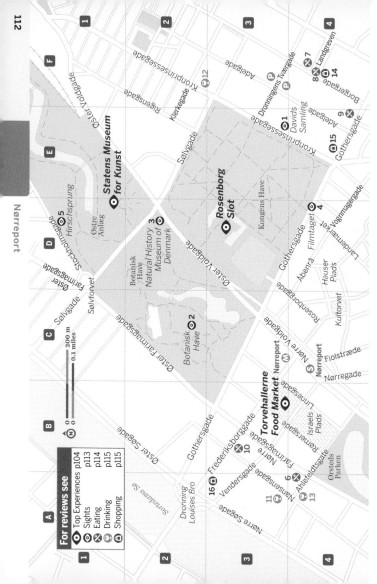

Nørreport

For reviews see
- ◎ Top Experiences p104
- ◉ Sights p113
- ✕ Eating p114
- ◎ Drinking p115
- ⓐ Shopping p115

0   200 m
0   0.1 miles

Øster Voldgade

Kronprinsessegade

Rigensgade

Adelgade

Klerkegade

Sølvgade

Rømersgade

Åbenrå

Statens Museum for Kunst ◎

Rosenborg Slot ◎

Hirschsprung ◎5

Østre Anlæg

Øster Farimagsgade

Stockholmsgade

Sølvgade

Botanisk Have **Natural History Museum of Denmark** ◎3

Botanisk Have ◎2

Øster Farimagsgade

Øster Voldgade

Kongens Have

Gothersgade

Rosenborggade

Dronningens Tværgade ◎1 Davids Samling

Kronprinsessegade

✕7 8⊗ⓐ14 Landgreven Borgergade

Adelgade ✕9

ⓐ15 Gothersgade

Filmtaget ◎ ◎4 Landemærket Vognmagergade

Hauser Plads

Kultorvet

Gothersgade

Norre Voldgade

Nørreport Ⓜ

Nørreport Ⓢ

Nørregade

Fiolstræde

Linnésgade

Torvehallerne Food Market ◎ Nørreport

Israels Plads

Frederiksborggade ✕⊗10

Nørre Farimagsgade

Vendersgade ✕6

Nansensgade

✕11

ⓐ16

ⓐ13

Gothersgade

Øster Søgade

Nørre Søgade

Anfeldtsgate

Ørsteds Parken

Dronning Louises Bro

Sortedams Sø

Sights

Davids Samling MUSEUM

1 ⊙ MAP P112, E3

Davids Samling is a wonderful curiosity housing Scandinavia's largest collections of Islamic art, including jewellery, ceramics and silk, and exquisite works such as an Egyptian rock crystal jug from CE 1000 and a 500-year-old Indian dagger inlaid with rubies. And it doesn't end there, with an elegant selection of Danish, Dutch, English and French art, porcelain, silverware and furniture from the 17th to 19th centuries. (www.davidmus.dk)

Botanisk Have GARDENS

2 ⊙ MAP P112, C2

Restorative and romantic, Copenhagen's Botanic Garden lays claim to around 13,000 species of plant life – the largest collection in Denmark. Amble along tranquil trails, or escape to the tropics inside the 19th-century Palmehuset glasshouse, with rare and exotic fauna. Note the spiral stairs heading to the top dome. Admission (60kr) includes entry to the Butterfly House where 60 tropical species flutter among guests and cactuses. (www.botanik.snm.ku.dk)

Natural History Museum of Denmark MUSEUM

3 ⊙ MAP P112, D2

At the northeast corner of the Botanic Garden, Denmark's Museum of Natural History hosts interesting exhibitions, with themes ranging from the Neanderthals to the glittering world of minerals and precious stones, including a 16-ton meteorite from outer space. In 2024, the museum is set to reopen in a state-of-the-art building in the Botanic Garden. The massive $160 million construction will span three exhibition floors underground. (www.geologi.snm.ku.dk)

Filmtaget CULTURAL CENTRE

4 ⊙ MAP P112, D4

Denmark is home to the Dogme 95 film movement, Lars von Trier, Mads Mikkelsen and award-winning films like *Drunk* and *Hævnen* – thanks to the Danish Film Institute housed in a five-floor building overlooking the King's Garden. As of late 2023, its rooftop will open with a 128-seat outdoor cinema and an exhibition on Danish film history inside seven film pavilions. (www.filmtaget.dk)

Hirschsprung MUSEUM

5 ⊙ MAP P112, D1

Dedicated to Danish art of the 19th and early 20th centuries, Hirschsprungske is a little jewel box of a gallery, full of wonderful surprises for art lovers unfamiliar with the classic era of Danish oil painting. Originally the private holdings of tobacco magnate Heinrich Hirschsprung, it contains works by Golden Age painters such as Christen Købke and CW Eckersberg, a notable selection by Skagen painters PS Krøyer and Anna and Michael Ancher, and works by the Danish symbolists and the Funen painters. (www.hirschsprung.dk)

Eating

Høst
NEW NORDIC $$$

6 ❌ MAP P112, A4

Høst's popularity is easy to understand: award-winning interiors and New Nordic food that's fabulous and filling. The set menu is superb, with smaller 'surprise dishes' thrown in and evocative creations like birch-smoked scallops with horseradish and green beans, or a joyful blueberry sorbet paired with Norwegian brown cheese and crispy caramel. (www.cofoco.dk/en/restaurants/hoest)

Pluto
DANISH $$$

7 ❌ MAP P112, F4

Loud, convivial Pluto is not short of friends, and for good reason: superfun soundtrack, attentive staff and beautiful, simple dishes by respected local chef Rasmus Oubæk. Whether it's flawlessly seared cod with seasonal carrots or a side of new potatoes, funky truffles and green beans in a mussel broth, the family-style menu is all about letting the produce sing. (www.restaurantpluto.dk midnight)

Gasoline Grill on Landgreven
BURGERS $

8 ❌ MAP P112, F4

Copenhagen's fast-emerging hamburger empire was founded inside the gas station on Landgreven in 2016. Now with six additional take-out locations, the original Gasoline Grill remains a pilgrimage among fans. The menu is straightforward: four burgers (one vegetarian), fries with a choice of toppings and homemade dips, and two desserts.

The place closes when the burgers run out; usually around 7pm. (Go at lunch to avoid disappointment.) (www.gasolinegrill.com)

Atelier September
CAFE $

9 ❌ MAP P112, E4

It might look like a *Vogue* photo shoot with its white-on-white interior and vintage glass ceiling (typical of old Danish pharmacies), but Atelier September is very much a cafe. Kitted out in vintage exhibition posters and communal tables, it sells gorgeous espresso and simple, inspired edibles. (www.atelierseptember.dk)

Slurp Ramen Joint
RAMEN $$

10 ❌ MAP P112, B3

It makes sense that white-tile, pink-neon Slurp serves Copenhagen's best ramen: head chef Philipp Inreiter once worked at cult-status Tokyo ramen-joint Hototogisu. The deeply flavoursome chicken-and-pork bone broth is cooked for more than eight hours, while noodles are made in-house with a pinch of freshly ground rye for added depth. Best of the trio of options (which includes a vegetarian ramen) is the shoyu.

Slurp is small, hugely popular and has a no-reservations policy:

go as close to opening as possible and get your name on the waiting list. (www.slurpramen.dk)

Drinking

Bibendum
WINE BAR

11 🏠 MAP P112, A3

In a snug, rustic cellar on Nansensgade, Bibendum is an oenophile's best friend. While the savvy wine list offers over 30 wines by the glass, always ask the barkeeps what's off the menu. The vibe is intimate but relaxed and the menu of small plates (80kr to 160kr) simply gorgeous. (www.bibendum.dk)

Culture Box
CLUB

12 🏠 MAP P112, F2

Electronica connoisseurs swarm to Culture Box, known for its impressive local and international DJ lineups and sharp sessions of electro, techno, house and drum'n'bass. The club is divided into three spaces: preclubbing Culture Box Bar, intimate club space Red Box, and heavyweight Black Box, where big-name DJs play the massive sound system. (www.culture-box.com)

Bankeråt
BAR

13 🏠 MAP P112, A4

Kooky, attitude-free Bankeråt is decorated with taxidermic animals in outlandish get-ups – yes, there's even a ram in period costume. The man behind it all is local artist Filip V Jensen. But is it art? Debate this, and the mouth-shaped urinals, over a local craft beer. (www.bankeraat.dk)

Shopping

Tranquebar
BOOKS

14 🔒 MAP P112, F4

Named after a port town in India, with strong ties to Denmark, the early profile of Tranquebar was strictly in guidebooks. The theme has since moved to world literature with a strong sense of place, organised into countries and regions. Hemingway, for instance, is found under 'Paris' and 'Tanzania'. Not far from the shelf for Ethiopia is, appropriately, a coffee bar. (www.tranquebar.net)

Stine Goya
FASHION & ACCESSORIES

15 🔒 MAP P112, E4

The winner of numerous prestigious design awards, Stine Goya is one of Denmark's hottest names in women's fashion. What makes her collections unique is the ability to marry clean Nordic simplicity with quirky details. Memorable recent offerings include silky 'oversized' frocks printed with painted human faces. Not cheap but highly collectible. (www.stinegoya.com

Maduro
HOMEWARES

16 🔒 MAP P112, A3

Maduro owner Jeppe Maduro Hirsch handpicks the eclectic mix of beautiful objects, from ceramic plates, cups and vases, to quirky lamps, jewellery and fridge magnets. There's a fine selection of posters and prints from the likes of Kortkartellet, Michelle Carslund and Sivellink. (www.maduro.dk)

Explore

Nørrebro

Gritty Nørrebro subverts the Nordic stereotype with its dense, sexy collection of art-clad 19th-century tenements, multicultural crowds and thronging cafes and bars. Despite being home to Assistens Kirkegård – the final resting place of Hans Christian Andersen – this corner of the city is less about sights and more about independent craft stores and galleries, craft beers and kaleidoscopic street life.

The Short List

○ **Assistens Kirkegård (p121)** Picnic among late Danish legends in an enchanting old cemetery.

○ **Silberbauers Bistro (p121)** Slurp fresh seafood and French wines at a loud, convivial stalwart.

○ **Coffee Collective (p124)** Sip a sustainable single origin brew on one of the city's coolest neighbourhood strips.

○ **Bæst (p121)** Tuck into house-made charcuterie, cheese and wood-fired pizza perfection at Christian Puglisi's bustling local bistro.

○ **Brus (p123)** Taste-test out-of-the-box craft beers and kegged cocktails from rock-star indie brewer To Øl.

Getting There & Around

Ⓜ The M3 Cityring line stops at Nørrebros Runddel by Assistens Kirkegård.

🚌 Routes 5C and 350S connect the city centre to Nørrebro. Both routes run along Nørrebrogade, Nørrebro's main thoroughfare.

Nørrebro Map on p120

Assistens Kirkegård (p121) OLIVER FOERSTNER/SHUTTERSTOCK ©

Walking Tour 🥾

Nørrebro Soul

Nørrebro is Copenhagen's creative heart, a multiethnic enclave splashed with quirky parks and street art, intriguing workshops and studios, as well as the city's most beautiful eternal resting place. So tie up those sneakers and hit the pavement for red squares and bulls, giant birds and tankers, and a shady street turned good.

Start The Red Square
Ⓜ M3 to Nørrebro
End Jægersborggade
Ⓜ M3 to Nørrebro Runddel
Length 2km; 1.5 hours

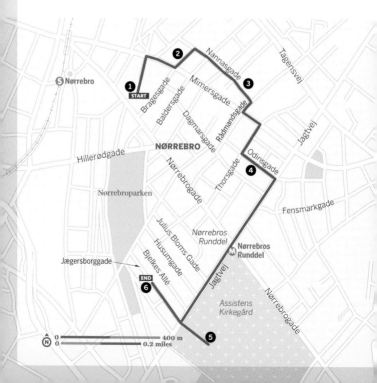

❶ The Red Square

The name of this square is borrowed, along with everything else: Russian neon signs, swings from Iraq and benches from Brazil. Strike onwards to the 'Black Market', the second part of the 1km-long park **Superkilen** (p121), where things turn striped and black-and-white – to the TikToker's delight.

❷ Basco5 Mural

Head east along Mimersgade, turning left into Bragesgade. On the side of number 35 is a **street art mural** by Copenhagen artist Nils Blishen, better known as Basco5. Birds, bearded men and a round, cartoonish style are all trademarks of the artist's work.

❸ BaNanna Park

Turn right into Nannasgade and walk 250m to oil-refinery-turned-playground **BaNanna Park**. Its striking gateway is a 14m-high climbing wall, popular with eye-candy locals and open to all (BYO climbing equipment).

❹ Odinsgade Murals

Step right into Rådmandsgade, left into Mimersgade, and right again into Thorsgade. Two blocks ahead is Odinsgade. The whimsical mural on the side of number 17 is by Simon Hjermind Jensen, Anne Sofie Madsen and Claus Frederiksen. The adjacent tanker mural uses existing architectural features to dramatic effect.

❺ Assistens Kirkegård

At Jagvej, turn right, and continue to hallowed **Assistens Kirkegård** (p121). In 2013 the cemetery created a 75-sq-metre burial plot for the city's homeless, complete with a bronze sculpture by artist Leif Sylvester. Some 50m further into the park is another large totem-like tombstone made by Sylvester with the epitaph *Det var det* – 'That was it'.

❻ Jægersborggade

Directly opposite Assistens Kirkegård, Jægersborggade is a vibrant hub of craft studios, boutiques and eating spots. At no 45, **Vanishing Point** (p125) showcases quirky local ceramics, jewellery, handmade knits, quilts and engaging, limited-edition prints, much of it made on site. At No 48, **Gågron!** (p125) peddles design-literate everyday products with a conscience.

✕ Take a Break

End your saunter with liquid-nitrogen ice cream at **Istid** (p122).

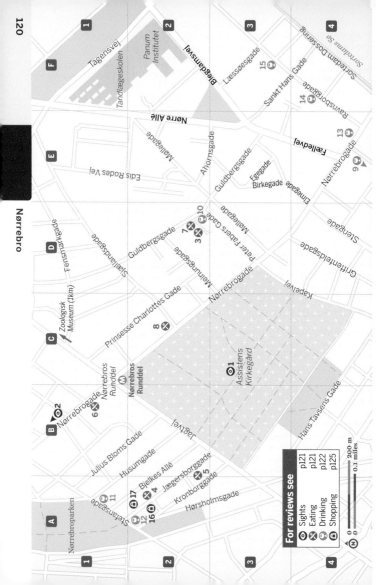

For reviews see

⊙ Sights	p121
✕ Eating	p121
● Drinking	p122
🛍 Shopping	p125

0 200 m
0 0.1 miles

Tagensvej

Tandlægeskolen

Panum
Institutet

Ble`g`damsvej

Læssøesgade

15

Sankt Hans Gade

Ravnsborggade

14

Nørre Allé

Møllegade

Anhornsgade

Guldbergsgade

Egegade

Birkegade

Elmegade

Fælledvej

13

Nørrebrogade

9

Edis Rodes Vej

Stengade

Griffenfeldsgade

Sjællandsgade

Fensmarkgade

Guldbergsgade

Peter Fabers Gade

Møllegade

7
3
10

Meinungsgade

Nørrebrogade

Kapelvej

Zoologisk
Museum (1km)

Prinsesse Charlottes Gade

Nørrebrogade

8

⊙1
Assistens
Kirkegård

Hans Tavsens Gade

Nørrebros
Runddel

Nørrebros Runddel

Nørrebrogade

6

Jagtvej

Julius Bloms Gade

Husumgade

Bjelkes Allé

17

4

Jægersborggade

5

Kronborggade

Hørsholmsgade

Nørrebroparken

Stefansgade

11

12

16

2

Nørrebrogade

Sights

Assistens Kirkegård

CEMETERY

1 MAP P120, C3

You'll find some of Denmark's most celebrated citizens at this famous cemetery, including philosopher Søren Kierkegaard, physicist Niels Bohr, author Hans Christian Andersen and artists Jens Juel, Christen Købke and CW Eckersberg. It's a wonderfully atmospheric place to wander around – as much a park and garden as it is a graveyard. A good place to start is at the main entrance on Kapelvej, where you can usually find fold-out maps of the cemetery and its notable burial sites. (www.assistens.dk)

Superkilen

PARK

2 MAP P120, B1

The 1km-long Superkilen park is a hyper-playful ode to the area's multicultural fabric, showcasing public-square objects sourced from around the globe. Items include a tile fountain from Morocco, bollards from Ghana and swing chairs from Baghdad, as well as neon signs from Russia and China. Even the benches, manhole covers and rubbish bins hail from foreign lands. The *Bibliotek* public library, by the Red Square, has won awards for interior design.

Local Life

It might sound macabre, but historic cemetery **Assistens Kirkegård** is a popular picnic and sunbathing spot in the warmer months. Graced with leafy, tranquil nooks, it's a blissful spot to spend a lazy afternoon reading a good book or simply contemplating the beauty of life...and maybe cheese.

Eating

Bæst

ITALIAN $$

3 MAP P120, D2

Owned by powerhouse Italo-Scandi chef Christian Puglisi, Bæst remains hot years after its 2014 launch. Charcuterie, cheese and competent woodfired pizzas are the draw-cards here. Much of the produce is organic, and both the commendable charcuterie and hand-stretched mozzarella are made upstairs (the latter made using jersey milk from Bæest's own farm). To fully appreciate its repertoire, opt for the sharing menu (small/large 375/450kr). (www.baest.dk)

Silberbauers Bistro

SEAFOOD $$

4 MAP P120, A2

The French-style Silberbauers Bistro has established itself as a top choice for fish and shellfish in

Copenhagen, serving a catch literally hauled the same day. Some 30 tables with red-checkered tableware fill up the easygoing venue and the atmosphere is neighbourly. Lunch is only on weekends. Book ahead. (www.silberbauers.dk)

Istid   ICE CREAM $

5 🍴 MAP P120, B2

Five Kitchenaid mixers, with five different ice-cream flavours, line the counter of this elegant ice-cream vendor on the vibrant boutique street Jægerborggade. Upon order, the ingredients are turned into frozen form with the use of liquid nitrogen – for smooth and silky texture – and served in homemade cardamom waffles. Closed over winter. (www.istid.dk)

Grums   BREAKFAST $

6 🍴 MAP P120, B1

Polaroids on the wall. Monstera in the window. Chess board by the record player. Grums ticks the boxes of a hipster coffee shop, and is popular among Nørrebro's laptop class. Open from 7.30am, breakfast leans towards quality over quantity: crispy croissants, grilled cheese or a bowl of *skyr* (strained yoghurt) with rhubarb jam and granola.

Mirabelle   CAFE $$

7 🍴 MAP P120, D2

Decked out with bold geometric floor tiles, artisan bakery-cafe Mirabelle is owned by Michelin-lauded chef Christian Puglisi, who also owns popular restaurant Bæst next door. It's a slick, contemporary spot for made-from-scratch pastries, simple breakfast bites like eggs Benedict, and a short menu of Italo-centric lunch and dinner dishes, including house-made charcuterie, cheeses and organic-flour pasta. Good coffee to boot. (www.mirabelle-bakery.dk)

Turning Chicken   MIDDLE EASTERN $

8 🍴 MAP P120, C2

Ignore the outside poster of a female model awkwardly holding a German bratwurst *and* the colour-faded images of top dishes: the real deal looks much better and locals know it. The wide-ranging style reflects the migrant route of its Turkish-born owner Imam Gür – the durum bread is made 'the German way' and the falafel bowls are topped with Danish cabbage.

Drinking

Blågårds Apotek   BAR

9 🍷 MAP P120, E4

The bar table was once a pharmacy counter, but not every uplifting spirit served here today is in liquid form. It's in the music, too. The venue is best known for jazz, with a jam every Monday and Wednesday, but over the weekends all kinds of names take to the stage. Over summer, concerts also take place outside, by the lively street of Blågårdsgade. (www.kroteket.dk)

Eco Capital

While some Western governments continue to debate the veracity of climate-change science, Denmark gets on with innovative, sustainable business. Indeed, the Danish capital is well on its way to becoming the world's first carbon neutral capital, although the original goal of reaching target by 2025 had to be revised.

Green Mobility

Implementation of the CPH 2025 Climate Plan's focus areas – energy consumption, energy production, green mobility and city-administration initiatives – is visible across the city. Since 2019, the metro system has doubled the number of stations with the opening of two new lines: the 5.5km-long city-circle route M3 and the suburban harbour line M4. In the meantime, hundreds of city buses have been upgraded with special air filters that cut pollution by 95%.

Denmark's capital is crisscrossed by over 400km of safe, connected bike paths, and even the traffic lights are programmed to give cyclists precedence in peak hour. Less than 30% of local households own a car and the number of bikes trumps the number of cars in the city centre.

Ditching the Dirt

Ready to remind Copenhageners of the pressing nature of environmental matters is the city's new waste-to-energy plant, Copenhill. Designed by local architecture firm Bjarke Ingels Group (BIG), the world's cleanest incineration plant, providing energy to 90,000 households, works also as a...recreational facility! On any given day, you are likely to see skiers or snowboarders go down the 450m green roof, while others come for the view.

For Copenhagen, this also involves a hand from its harbour. City energy utility company HOFOR uses an innovative district cooling system that uses local seawater to provide cooling services to businesses in central Copenhagen. The system saves around 70% of the energy used by traditional air-conditioning systems. Copenhagen harbour itself is an environmental success story: the once heavily polluted waterway is now clean enough for swimming.

Brus

MICROBREWERY

10 MAP P120, D2

What was once a locomotive factory is now a huge, sleek, hip brewpub. The world-renowned microbrewery behind it is To Øl, and the bar's 30-plus taps offer a rotating selection of To Øl

Vilhelm Dahlerup & Dronning Louises Bro

It is said that no single architect has contributed to Copenhagen's current look as much as Vilhelm Dahlerup (1836–1907). The city's leading architect of the late 19th century, Dahlerup borrowed from a broad spectrum of European Renaissance influences. His Historicist style of architecture shines especially bright in Ny Carlsberg Glyptotek and the glorious Det Kongelige Teater, two exceptional works in a long list of buildings that also include the Hotel d'Angleterre, Pantomime Theatre at Tivoli Gardens, Carlsberg Brewery and Statens Museum for Kunst.

The influence of the French Empire style is palpable in Dahlerup's **Dronning Louises Bro**, the bridge connecting central Copenhagen to Nørrebro. Dating from 1887, its namesake is Queen Louise, wife of Christian IX. The current crossing succeeds two earlier versions: a wooden bridge built in the 16th century and a combined bridge-dam constructed a century later. In the evening, the bridge offers a prime-time view of Nørrebrø's famous neon lights; the best-loved of them is the Irma hen, laying electric eggs since 1953.

standards and small-batch specials, as well as eight on-tap cocktails. The barkeeps are affable and happy to let you sample different options before you commit. (www.tapperietbrus.dk)

Mikkeller & Friends   MICROBREWERY

11 🚇 MAP P120, A1

Looking suitably cool with its turquoise floors and pale ribbed wood, Mikkeller & Friends is a joint venture of Mikkeller and Denmark's largest craft brewers. Beer geeks go gaga over the 40 artisan draft beers and circa 100 bottled varieties, which might include a chipotle porter or an imperial stout aged in tequila

barrels. Overwhelmed? Try the Passion Pool. (www.mikkeller.dk/location/mikkeller-friends)

Coffee Collective   COFFEE

12 🚇 MAP P120, A2

Copenhagen's most prolific microroastery, Coffee Collective has helped revolutionise the city's coffee culture. Head in for rich, complex cups of caffeinated magic. The baristas are passionate about their single-origin beans and the venue itself sits at one end of creative Jægersborggade in Nørrebro. There are several other outlets, including at gourmet food market Torvehallerne KBH (p110). (www.coffeecollective.dk)

Kassen   BAR

13 🚇 MAP P120, E4

Loud, sticky Kassen sends livers packing with its dirt-cheap drinks and happy-hour specials (80kr cocktails, anyone?). Guzzle unlimited drinks on Thursdays for 250kr, with two-for-one deals running the rest of the week until 9pm. Cocktail choices are stock-standard and a little sweet, but think of the change in your pocket. (www.kassen.dk)

Kind of Blue   BAR

14 🚇 MAP P120, F4

Chandeliers, heady perfume and walls painted a hypnotic 1950s blue: the spirit of the Deep South runs deep at intimate Kind of Blue. Named after the Miles Davis album, it's never short of a late-night hipster crowd, kicking back porters and drinking in owner Claus' personal collection of soul-stirring jazz, blues and folk. You'll find it on Nørrebro's bar-packed Ravnsborggade. (www.kindofblue.dk)

Nørrebro Bryghus   BREWERY

15 🚇 MAP P120, F3

This now-classic brewery kickstarted the microbrewing craze more than a decade ago. While its in-house restaurant serves a decent lunchtime burger as well as fancier New Nordic dishes in the evening, head here for the beers, including the brewery's organic draught beer and a string of fantastic bottled options, from pale and brown ales to 'The Evil', a malty, subtly smokey, imperial porter. (www.noerrebrobryghus.dk)

Shopping

Vanishing Point   HANDICRAFTS

16 🔒 MAP P120, A2

On trendy Jægersborggade, Vanishing Point is a contemporary craft shop and studio showcasing quirky ceramics, unique jewellery, handmade knits and quilts, as well as engaging, limited-edition prints. Most items are created on site, while some are the result of a collaboration with nonprofits around the world. The aim: to inspire a sustainable and playful lifestyle through nature, traditional craft techniques and humour. (www.vanishing-point.dk)

Gågrøn!   HOMEWARES

17 🔒 MAP P120, A2

Gågron! peddles design-literate products with a conscience. The focus is on natural fibres and sustainable, recycled and upcycled materials, transformed into simple, stylish products for everyday use. Stock up on everything from kooky animal-shaped cutting boards and stylish cedarwood serving trays to aprons and toiletry bags made with organic cotton. (www.gagron.dk)

Walking Tour 🥾

Østerbro

Detractors might call it 'white bread' and boring, but salubrious Østerbro has some satisfying urban surprises, including heritage-listed architecture and a cinema-turned–design Valhalla. The neighbourhood's name means 'East Gate', a reference to the city's old eastern entrance. These days it's an area best known for its resident media stars, academics and slew of foreign embassies.

Getting There

Start Sortedams Sø

End Fischer

Length 2.5km; 2 hours

Ⓜ M3 to Østerport

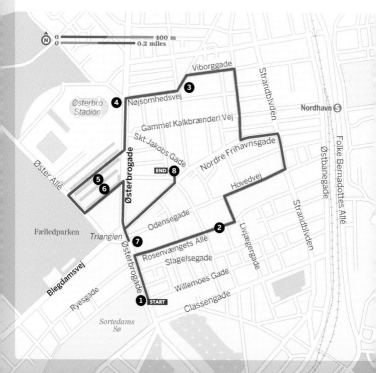

❶ Sortedams Sø

Sortedams Sø (Black Dam Lake) is the most northerly of Copenhagen's trio of central lakes. It's popular with joggers and flâneurs, and is a good spot to sit and reflect.

❷ Rosenvænget

Bordered by Rosenvængets Sideallé, Strandboulevarden, Holsteinsgade and Nordre Frihavnsgade, Rosenvænget is the city's oldest suburban development, established in the mid-19th century. Rosenvængets Allé 46 was designed by Vilhelm Dahlerup, creator of Ny Carlsberg Glyptotek.

❸ Pixie

Strung with colourful lights, boho cafe **Pixie** (www.cafepixie.dk) looks straight off the streets of Buenos Aires. Inside it's a *hyggelig* (cosy) affair with French furniture and candlelight.

❹ Juno the Bakery

Make a default stop at the long line outside Juno the Bakery, serving pistachio croissants, cardamom buns and *wienerbrød* ('Viennese bread'; Danish pastries) straight from the oven Wednesday to Sunday.

❺ Brumleby

Celebrated Danish writers Martin Andersen Nexø *(Pelle the Conqueror)* and Peter Høeg *(Miss Smilla's Feeling for Snow)* have both called Brumleby home. A heritage-listed combo of yellow-and-white row-housing and cosy gardens, the residential enclave was built to better house the poor after the 1853 cholera epidemic.

❻ Olufsvej

Technicolour Olufsvej is lined with 19th-century workers' abodes in a multitude of shades. These days, the properties are home to a number of well-known journalists.

❼ Bahne Trianglen

Sprawling **Bahne Trianglen** (www.bahne.dk) bursts with must-have design objects, from statement bowls and glassware to wooden toys, clothes and cushions. The space was once a cinema.

❽ Fischer

Another reformed local is **Fischer** (www.hosfischer.dk), a former worker's bar turned neighbourly trattoria. It makes sense that the Italian grub is so good, given that owner and head chef David Fischer worked the kitchen at Rome's Michelin-starred La Pergola.

Explore

Vesterbro

Once best known for butchers and sex workers, Vesterbro is now the epicentre of Copenhagen cool. The neighbourhood's hottest corner remains Kødbyen (Meat City), a still-functioning Meatpacking District laced with buzzing eateries, bars, galleries and music venues. Istedgade mixes porn shops with vintage boutiques and ethnic groceries, while further north lies continental Værnedamsvej.

The Short List

○ **V1 Gallery (p134)** Catch an exhibition of edgy contemporary art in the pumping Meatpacking District.

○ **Kødbyens Fiskebar (p136)** Find sustenance in wild-caught fish, foraged herbs and low-intervention wines in a slick factory conversion.

○ **Lidkoeb (p137)** Sip reconfigured cocktails and cognoscenti whiskies in a sneaky, multilevel drinking den.

○ **Vega (p138)** Rock out to on-point indie music acts in a mid-century building by architect Vilhelm Lauritzen.

○ **BaneGaarden (p135)** Discover the surprise location of Copenhagen's greenest street-food market hidden by the railway tracks.

Getting There & Around

🚌 Routes 6A and 26 run along Vesterbrogade to Frederiksberg Have. Route 9A runs along Gammel Kongevej, connecting Vesterbro to Slotsholmen and Christianshavn.

🚌 Kødbyen lies 500m southwest of Central Station.

Vesterbro Map on p132

Fleisch (p136) OLIVER FOERSTNER/SHUTTERSTOCK ©

Continental Værnedamsvej

Copenhagers have a soft spot for Værnedamsvej, a sassy little strip they commonly compare to the side streets of Paris. Gallic or not, it is one of Vesterbro's most appealing pockets, dotted with specialist cheese and wine shops, cafes and bistros, petite boutiques and an unmistakably easy, local vibe. Some shops close on the weekends, so head in during the week for the full experience.

Walk Facts

Start Granola

End Frederiksberg Allé

Length 600m; 1.5km if completing Frederiksberg Allé

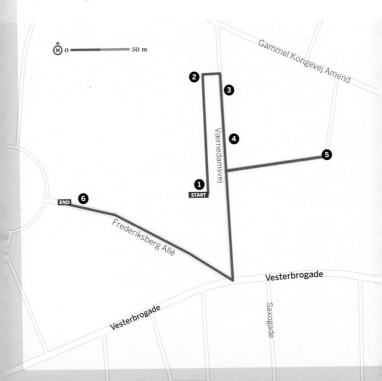

❶ Granola

Granola (www.granola.dk) is a staple of Copenhagen's brunch scene, with a cute general-store–inspired fitout.

❷ Juuls Vin og Spiritus

Vintage wine shop **Juuls Vin og Spiritus** (www.juuls.dk) sells some thirst-inducing drops, including spicy, fruity Brøndum akvavit and the organic Radius gin from southern Denmark.

❸ Falernum

Worn floorboards and chairs, bottled-lined shelves and soothing tunes give wine bar **Falernum** (www.falernum.dk) a deliciously moody air. You'll find around 40 wines by the glass alone, as well as boutique beers, coffee and a simple, seasonal menu of sharing plates like osso buco with roasted artichokes and onions, as well as cheeses and charcuterie.

❹ Samsøe & Samsøe

Originating from the Latin Quarter, **Samsøe & Samsøe** (www.samsoe. com) is well known for its contemporary threads for guys and girls. This is a label not afraid of unique patterns, colour and detailing, and the range includes supremely comfortable sweat tops, tees and denim, as well as sharper shirts, jackets, frocks and outerwear.

❺ Mads Nørgaard – Supermarket

Mads Nørgaard (www.madsnor gaard.com), Copenhagen's famous clothes brand, has a 'supermarket' at Tullinsgade. In more mundane terms, the supermarket is an outlet store, keeping up with Mads Nørgaard's foundational mission of 'slowing down' the fashion industry with quality and classic design. Seasoned collections – for men, women and kids – are half-priced, typically.

❻ Frederiksberg Allé

Goodbye, Copenhagen. The boulevard of Frederiksberg Allé is the border crossing of Frederiksberg, the municipality of low taxes and high trees: by local law all residents must be able to see a tree outside any window and no healthy tree over the age of 25 can be cut down. The avenue is 1km long, with a maze tucked inside Frederiksberg Have on the other end.

For reviews see

⊙	Sights	p134
⊗	Eating	p135
☻	Drinking	p137
☆	Entertainment	p138
🔒	Shopping	p139

N

0 _____ 200 m
0 _____ 0.1 miles

Gammel Kongevej

Amend

Frederiksberg Allé

Sankt
Thomas
Plads

Frederiksberg Allé

Værnedamsvej

⊕17

Kingosgade

Vesterbrogade

FREDERIKSBERG

Valdemarsgade

Oehlenschlægersgade

Platanvej

Vesterbrogade

Sundevedsgade

Vesterfælledvej

Amerikavej

Tøndergade

Hedebygade

Enghavevej

Matthæusgade

Frederiksstadsgade

Rejsbygade

Haderslevgade

Istedgade

⊕16

Saxogade

Lyrskovgade

15☆

Oehlenschlægersgade

Enghave
Plads
Ⓜ

Enghave
Plads

Valdemarsgade

Vesterfælledvej

Enghaveparken

Haderslevgade

Flensborggade

Ny Carlsberg Vej

Alsgade

Slesvigsgade

Enghavevej

Sønder Blvd

Ingerslevgade

4⊗

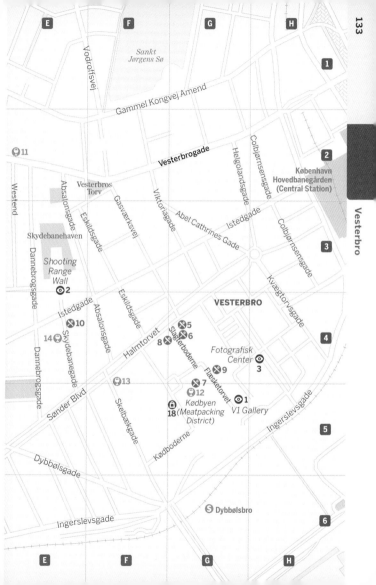

E

F

G

H

1

Vodroffsvej

Sankt
Jørgens Sø

Gammel Kongvej Amend

Vesterbrogade

Helgolandsgade

Colbjørnsensgade

2

**København
Hovedbanegården
(Central Station)**

11

Vesterbros
Torv

Gasværksvej

Eskildsgade

Absalonsgade

Viktoriagade

Abel Cathrines Gade

Istedgade

Colbjørnsensgade

Westend

Skydebanehaven

Dannebrogsgade

3

*Shooting
Range
Wall*
2

Istedgade

Eskildsgade

Absalonsgade

Halmtorvet

Kvægtorvsgade

VESTERBRO

4

10

14

Skydebanegade

8

5
6

Slagterboderne

*Fotografisk
Center*
3

Dannebrogsgade

Sønder Blvd

13

Skelbækgade

Flæsketorvet

9

7

12

18
*Kødbyen
(Meatpacking
District)*

1

V1 Gallery

Ingerslevsgade

5

Dybbølsgade

Kødboderne

Ingerslevsgade

S **Dybbølsbro**

6

E

F

G

H

Sights

V1 Gallery

GALLERY

1 MAP P132, G5

Part of the Kødbyen (Vester-bro's 'Meatpacking District'), V1 is one of Copenhagen's most progressive art galleries. Cast your eye on fresh work from both emerging and established local and foreign artists. Some of the world's hottest names in street and graffiti art have exhibited here, from Britain's Banksy to the USA's Todd James and Lydia Fong (aka Barry McGee). (www. v1gallery.com)

Street Art

Both Vesterbro and Frederiks-berg are home to some huge, spectacular street-art murals. Many of these cover the side walls of semidetached apart-ment buildings. In Vesterbro, honourable mentions go to Irish artist Conor Harrington's period piece at Tullingsgade 21, Brooklynite Maya Hayuk's geometric statement at Saxogade 7, Belgian art-ist Roa's furry critters at Gasværksvej 34 and Chinese artist DALeast's giant bird at Oehlenschlægersgade 76. In Frederiksberg, don't miss homegrown Martin Bigum's storybook work at Falkoner Allé 30.

Shooting Range Wall

HISTORIC SITE

2 MAP P132, E3

In a cul-de-sac off Istedgade is this imposing red-brick wall, its gate leading to the delightful Skydebanehaven (Shooting Range Gardens). While it might look medieval, the wall dates to 1887. At the time, this was the site of the Royal Copenhagen Shooting Society and the wall was built to protect locals from stray bullets. The club's target was parrot shaped, leading to the popular Danish saying 'You've shot the parrot there', used to refer to someone's good fortune. Today, the playground pays tribute to this past with a parrot-shaped slide.

Fotografisk Center

GALLERY

3 MAP P132, H4

Hidden away in a warehouse in the 'brown-brick' section of the Meat-packing District, the Fotografisk Center has rotating exhibitions of contemporary photography and related media, including video art and film. Both Danish and interna-tional artists are represented, in either solo or group shows.

Fotografisk Center also hosts the recurring series *Ung dansk fotografi* (Young Danish Photog-raphy). The gallery's founder is prolific Danish photographer and gallerist Lars Schwander. (www. fotografiskcenter.dk)

CAROLINE HADAMITZKY/LONELY PLANET ©

Paté Paté

Eating

BaneGaarden

STREET FOOD $$

4 MAP P132, A6

To enter the street-food market BaneGaarden, pass the railway tracks via a pedestrian underpass and continue towards a small labyrinth. On the other end awaits the rustic courtyard, tucked between warehouses formerly occupied by railway repair workers. The fixers of today, however, serve Japanese fusion to South American soul food – from a total of seven stalls.

Closed from October to April, except the permanent new Nordic restaurant **Lade 609**. (www.banegaarden.com)

Paté Paté

INTERNATIONAL $$

5 MAP P132, G4

This pâté-factory-turned-restaurant/wine bar gives a modern twist to Euro classics. The competent, regularly changing menu is designed for sharing, with smaller dishes like organic Danish burrata with salted courgette, spring onions, chilli, basil and walnuts, or veal tartare with harissa, mustard-pickled shallots and dukkah. Hip and bustling, yet refreshingly convivial, bonus extras include clued-in staff, a diverse wine list and solo-diner-friendly bar seating. (www.patepate.dk)

Fleisch
DANISH $$$

6 ✶ MAP P132, G4

The Meatpacking District is an appropriate setting for Fleisch – a white-tiled butcher shop, bar and restaurant combined. The place serves simple, rustic food, with a lunchtime focus on smørrebrød and a dinnertime choice of two good-value set menus. *Most* dishes hit the mark, among them a combination of tartare, unripened green peach and potato crisps quirkily served on a hollowed-out bone. (www.fleisch.dk)

Kødbyens Fiskebar
SEAFOOD $$$

7 ✶ MAP P132, G4

Concrete floors, industrial tiling and a 1000-litre aquarium meet impeccable seafood at this ever-popular, buzzy haunt, slap bang in Vesterbro's trendy Kødbyen. Ditch the mains for three or four starters. Standouts include the oysters and lobster with beer meringue, as well as the dainty, delicate razor clams, served on a crisp rice-paper 'shell'. (www. fiskebaren.dk)

Hija de Sanchez
MEXICAN $

8 ✶ MAP P132, F4

Hija de Sanchez serves up fresh, authentic tacos in the Meatpacking District. Expect three rotating varieties daily, from traditional choices like *carnitas* and *al pastor* to 'El Paul' – crispy fish skin with gooseberry salsa. There's always a vegetarian option, as well as homemade Mexican beverages like *tepache* (fermented pineapple juice). Chicago-native chef-owner Rosio Sánchez hails from renowned local restaurant noma, so there's serious culinary cred. (www.hijadesanchez.dk)

WarPigs
BARBECUE $$

9 ✶ MAP P132, G4

Loud, rocking WarPigs satiates carnivores with lusty, American-style barbecue from Europe's biggest meat smokers (capable of smoking up to two tons of meat a day). Order at the counter, where you can mix and match meats and sides to create a personalised feed. There's also a kicking selection of beers brewed

Mikkeller Bar

ULF SVANE/LONELY PLANET ©

Beer Guide Top 3

Freddy's Bar Welcome to a traditional Danish bodega with massive ashtrays, the names of regulars carved on the table and the clock fixed at five in the afternoon. Choose between a lager or a classic, served in bottles.

Mikkeller Bar Denmark's craft-beer pioneer laid the foundation in Vesterbro when the school teacher Mikkel Bjergsø started home-brewing as a science experience and selling bottles at a beer shop owned by his twin brother Jeppe. The sour ales are my favourite. (www.mikkeller.dk)

Fermentoren The place to meet the people of Vesterbro, with a crowd of all ages united in their love for craft beer. With 24 draughts, the bar packs the best of Denmark's craft-beer scene. (p138)

Amanda Bomholt is a tour guide at Mie & Friends. @copenhagenbymie

in-house; the place doubles as a brewpub part-owned by local microbrewery **Mikkeller** (www.mikkeller.dk)

Siciliansk Is
ICE CREAM $

10 MAP P132, E4

Honing their skills in Sicily, gelato meisters Michael and David churn out Copenhagen's (dare we say Denmark's) best gelato. Lick yourself out on smooth, naturally flavoured options like strawberry, Sicilian blood orange and coconut. For a surprisingly smashing combo, try the *lakrids* (liquorice) with the Sicilian mandarin. *Buonissimo!* (www.sicilianskis.dk)

Drinking

Lidkoeb
COCKTAIL BAR

11 MAP P132, E2

Lidkoeb loves a game of hide-and-seek: follow the 'Lidkoeb' signs into the second, light-strung courtyard. Once found, this top-tier cocktail lounge rewards with passionate barkeeps and clever, seasonal libations. Slip into a Børge Mogensen chair and toast to Danish ingenuity with Nordic bar bites and seasonal drinks like the Freja's Champagne: a gin-based concoction with muddled fresh ginger, lemon and maraschino liqueur.

Extras include a dedicated whisky bar upstairs, open Friday and Saturday nights only. (www.lidkoeb.dk)

Mesteren & Lærlingen BAR

12 MAP P132, G5

In a previous life, Mesteren & Lærlingen was a slaughterhouse bodega. These days it's one of Copenhagen's in-the-know drinking holes, its tiled walls packing in an affable indie crowd of trucker caps and skinny jeans. Squeeze in and sip good spirits (including a decent mezcal selection) to DJ-spun soul, reggae, hip-hop and dance hall. Wi-fi is available if you ask politely.

Cykelslangen

Two of the Danes' greatest passions – design and cycling – meet in spectacular fashion with Cykelslangen, or Cycle Snake. Designed by local architects Dissing + Weitling, the 235m-long cycling path evokes a slender ribbon, its gently curving form contrasting dramatically against the area's block-like architecture. The elevated path winds its way from Bryggebro (Brygge Bridge) west to Fisketorvet Shopping Centre, delivering a cycling experience that's nothing short of whimsical. To reach the path on public transport, catch bus 34 to Fisketorvet Shopping Centre. The best way to reach it, however, is on a bike, as Cykelslangen is only accessible to cyclists.

Fermentoren CRAFT BEER

13 MAP P132, F4

Serious local beer fans flock to this cosy, candlelit, basement bar. Its 24 taps pour an ever-changing cast of interesting craft brews, both traditional and edgy. Look out for local brews from the likes of Evil Twin, Ghost and Gamma, as well as Fermentoren's own pale ale. Staff are extremely knowledgeable, offering expert advice without the attitude. (www.fermentoren.com)

Sort Kaffe & Vinyl CAFE

14 MAP P132, E4

This skinny little cafe/record store combo is a second home for Vesterbro's coffee cognoscenti. Join them for velvety espresso, hunt down that limited-edition Blaxploitation LP, or score a prized pavement seat and eye up the eye-candy regulars.

Entertainment

Vega LIVE MUSIC

15 MAP P132, B4

The daddy of Copenhagen's live-music venues, Vega hosts everyone from big-name rock, pop, blues and jazz acts to underground indie, hip-hop and electro up-and-comers. Gigs take place on either the main stage (Store Vega), small stage (Lille Vega) or the ground-floor Ideal Bar. Performance times vary; check the website. (www.vega.dk)

Shopping

Kyoto
FASHION & ACCESSORIES

16 🔒 MAP P132, D4

Unisex, multibrand Kyoto pulls cool hunters with its awesome edits of mostly Nordic labels: think hardy S.N.S. Herning knits, Wrench Monkey shirts, Norse Project tees, Acne Studios denim, as well as Libertine-Libertine and Rodebjer frocks. International interlopers include French labels A.P.C. and Kitsuné, while the cast of well-chosen accessories include statement sneakers, fragrances and slinky leather wallets. (www.kyoto.dk)

Dora
DESIGN

17 🔒 MAP P132, D2

If you're after a cactus-print bolster, a striking hand-poured bowl, or a hygge-scented candle partly made with organic beeswax, chances are you'll find it at Dora. This is one of the city's most eclectic design and gift shops, with harder-to-find objects for any room of the house. Look out for local design wares from the likes of Troels Flensted, Broste and Skandinavisk. (www.shopdora.dk)

CAROLINE HADAMITZKY/LONELY PLANET ©

Sort Kaffe & Vinyl

Motorious
FASHION & ACCESSORIES

18 🔒 MAP P132, G5

Customers reportedly walk away from this store thinking they ought to get a motorbike soon – or at least come back for that leather messenger bag. The style is flannel shirts, Blacksmith boots and beanie caps, carefully curated. The owners – who take turns running the store and fixing motorbikes next door – offer their help with a simple first-choice, 'Coffee?' (www.motorious.dk)

Walking Tour 🥾

Frederiksberg Have

Aspirational Copenhageners dream of a Frederiksberg address. Located directly west of Vesterbro, it's a moneyed district, laced with fin-de-siècle architecture, neighbourly bistros and leafy residential streets. It's here that you'll find the landscaped elegance of Frederiksberg Have and the architecturally notable Copenhagen Zoo, as well as one of Copenhagen's finest flea markets.

Getting There

Ⓜ Frederiksberg station is 300m north of Frederiksberg Rådhus.

🚌 Routes 9A and 31 pass the Rådhus.

🚲 Route 51, the Green Path, is a spectacular 8km ride from Nørrebro.

❶ Sokkelund

Classic **Sokkelund** (www.cafe-sokkelund.dk) is the quintessential neighbourhood brasserie, kitted out with leather banquettes, newspapers on hooks and handsome waiters in crisp white shirts.

❷ Frederiksberg Loppetorv

If it's Saturday, scour cult-status flea-market Frederiksberg Loppetorv. The neighbourhood's affluence is reflected in the quality of the goods, and seasoned treasure hunters head in early for the best finds. There's usually plenty of local and international fashion, with the odd Danish design collectible in the mix.

❸ Frederiksberg Have

Romantic Frederiksberg Have woos with its lakes and woodlands. Look out for the Chinese summerhouse pavilion, sometimes open for tea. Overlooking the park is Frederiksborg Slot, a former royal palace, now home to the Royal Danish Military Academy.

❹ Copenhagen Zoo

Perched on Frederiksberg (Frederik's Hill), **Copenhagen Zoo** (www.zoo.dk) rumbles with more than 2500 of nature's lovelies. The Panda House is the latest attraction, along with the Arctic Ring enclosure, allowing visitors to walk right through the polar-bear pool.

❺ Cisternerne

Below Søndermarken Park lurks Copenhagen's 19th-century water reservoir. These days it's best known as **Cisternerne** (www.cisternerne.dk), one of Copenhagen's most unusual art spaces. The gallery has one major exhibition each year – check the website.

❻ Carlsberg Brewery

Carlsberg Brewery was designed by architect Vilhelm Dahlerup. The brewery's **visitors centre** (www.visitcarlsberg.dk) explores the history of Danish beer from 1370 BCE, leading you past antique copper vats and the brewery's famous Jutland dray horses. A new visitors centre, years in the making, is due to open this year.

Worth a Trip 👓
Relax in Louisiana's Seaside Sculpture Garden

Even if you don't have a consuming passion for modern art, Denmark's outstanding **Louisiana Museum of Modern Art** *should be high on your 'to do' list. It's a striking modernist gallery, made up of four huge wings, which stretch across a sculpture-filled park, burrowing down into the hillside and nosing out again to wink at the sea (and Sweden).*

www.louisiana.dk

Permanent Collection

The museum's permanent collection, mainly postwar paintings and graphic art, covers everything from constructivism, CoBrA movement artists and minimalist art, to abstract expressionism, pop art and staged photography. Pablo Picasso, Francis Bacon and Alberto Giacometti are some of the international luminaries you'll come across inside, while prominent Danish artists include Asger Jorn, Carl-Henning Pedersen, Robert Jacobsen and Richard Mortensen.

Architecture

Danish architects Vilhelm Wohlert and Jørgen Bo spent several months walking around the grounds before deciding on their design for Louisiana. The result would be one of the country's finest examples of modernist architecture, a series of horizontal, light-washed buildings in harmony with their natural surroundings. The museum's three original buildings – completed in 1958 and known as the North Wing – are now accompanied by subsequent extensions. The seats in the Concert Hall are the work of the late designer Poul Kjaerholm.

Sculpture Garden

With views across the deep-blue Øresund to Sweden, Louisiana's arresting grounds are peppered with sculptures from some of the world's most venerated artists. You'll find works from the likes of Max Ernst, Louise Bourgeois, Joan Miró, Henry Moore and Jean Arp, each one positioned to interact with the environment surrounding it. Site-specific works include George Trakas' *Self Passage* and Richard Serra's *The Gate in the Gorge*.

★ Top Tips

○ Museum director Poul Erik Tøjner claims the decision he is most proud of is to extend weekday opening hours to 10pm. On a calm summer night, it's hard to disagree!

★ Getting There

The Louisiana is in Humlebæk, 35 minutes by train from Copenhagen. Depart from Copenhagen Central or Nørreport station with a Zone 8 ticket and get out at Humlebæk. Follow the signs for the 15-minute walk to the museum.

Catch bus 388 and get off at Humlebæk Strandvej/Louisiana

✕ After the Visit

Some 800m inland from the museum is a huge fruit and vegetable market operated by Aarstiderne, a leading meal-kit company, and a barn cafe. It's 1.5km back to the station via the wooden path marked 'Humblebæk Centre' – it starts on the field below the farm.

Survival Guide

Nyhavn (p77) STUDIOLASKA/SHUTTERSTOCK ©

Before You Go

Book Your Stay

○ The rates of some hostels and most midrange and top-end hotels are based on supply and demand, with daily fluctuations. In most cases, booking early guarantees the best deal.

○ Rooms in many of the most popular midrange hotels fill quickly so book in advance.

○ Copenhagen's hostels often fill early in summer so it's best to reserve ahead.

○ A Hostelling International (HI) Card will allow access to discounts on direct bookings with Danhostel and HI.

Useful Websites

○ **Copenhagen Visitors Centre** (www.visitcopenhagen.com) Can book last-minute accommodation for visitors.

○ **Eco Hotels** (www.ecohotels.com) Socially conscious booking site that lists sustainable

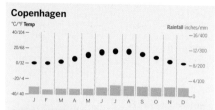

Copenhagen

When to Go

○ **Spring (Mar–May)** Tivoli Gardens open. Weather unpredictable.

○ **Summer (Jun–Aug)** Peak season, good weather and festivals.

○ **Autumn (Sep–Nov)** Fewer crowds, cultural events, Tivoli reopens around Halloween.

○ **Winter (Dec–Feb)** Short days, cold. Christmas lights, markets, *gløgg* (mulled wine).

hotels, charges low commissions and plants a tree for every booking.

○ **Lonely Planet** (lonelyplanet.com/denmark/copenhagen/hotels) Author-reviewed accommodation options.

Best Budget

○ **Generator Hostel** (www.staygenerator.com) Contemporary dorms, private rooms and a central location.

○ **Copenhagen Downtown Hostel** (www.copenhagendowntown.com) Gigs, city walks and free dinners in the historic centre.

○ **Urban House** (www.meininger-hotels.com) A Vesterbro hostel close to hip eateries and with its own tattoo parlour.

Best Midrange

○ **Hotel Alexandra** (www.hotelalexandra.dk) A chic yet homey hotel with cult-status furniture.

○ **Babette Guldsmeden** (www.guldsmedenhotels.com) Contemporary four-posters and a rooftop spa, near the Royal Palace.

○ **Hotel Danmark** (www.brochner-hotels.com) Elegant, wood-floored rooms and a rooftop terrace.

○ **CPH Living** (www. cphliving.com) A light-filled, Scandi-stylish floating hotel on Copenhagen harbour.

Best Top End

○ **Hotel d'Angleterre** (www.dangleterre. com) Near Nyhavn, history-steeped luxury, with rooms inspired by famous writers.

○ **Hotel Nimb** (www. nimb.dk) Unique luxury suites with views of a 19th-century pleasure garden.

○ **Radisson BLU Royal Hotel** (www.radissonblue.com) A mid-century icon created by design deity Arne Jacobsen.

○ **Villa Copenhagen** (www.villacopenhagen. com) Grand new hotel in a 19th-century building, with rooftop pool.

Arriving in Copenhagen

Copenhagen Airport

○ **Metro** The 24-hour metro (www.m.dk) runs every two to 20 minutes between the airport arrival terminal (the station is called Lufthavnen) and central Copenhagen. Alight at Kongens Nytorv for Nyhavn or to connect to the M3 City Circle (Cityringen) line. Journey time to Kongens Nytorv is 14 minutes.

○ **Train** Trains (www. dsb.dk) connect the airport arrival terminal to Copenhagen Central Station (Københavns Hovedbanegården, commonly known as København H) every 10 to 20 minutes. Journey time is 14 minutes.

○ **Taxi** Journey time from the airport to the city centre is about 20 minutes, depending on traffic. Expect to pay 250kr to 350kr.

Central Station

○ All regional and international trains arrive at and depart from Central Station located opposite Tivoli Gardens in the heart of the city. Trains run to the airport every 10 to 20 minutes, with less frequent services overnight.

Søndre Frihavn

○ Søndre Frihavn is 2km north of central Copenhagen and serves ferries to and from Oslo, Norway. The port is a 10- to 15-minute walk to Nordhavn station, where you can catch the M4 metro line or an S-train to the city centre.

Getting Around

Bus

○ City buses are frequent, convenient and run by Movia. If using a Rejsekort, tap on when boarding the bus and tap off when exiting. Buy single tickets in advance at 7-Eleven kiosks, from ticket vending machines at train and metro stations, or using the 'DOT Tickets' smartphone app. Single tickets can also be bought onboard from the driver (use small change).

○ Primary bus routes have an 'A' after their route number (eg: 1A, 2A) and run around the clock, every three to seven minutes in peak

Tickets & Passes

Copenhagen's bus, metro, S-train and Harbour Bus network has an integrated ticket system based on nine geographical zones. Most of your travel in the city will be within two zones. Travel between the city and airport covers three zones. The cheapest ticket *(billet)* covers two zones, offers unlimited transfers and is valid for one hour (adult 24kr, 12–15 years old 12kr). An adult with a valid ticket can take two children under the age of 12 free of charge.

Alternatively, you can purchase a **Rejsekort** (www.rejsekort.dk), a touch-on, touch-off smart card valid for all zones. Available from the Rejsekort machines at metro stations, Central Station or the airport. Various ticket types (including single tickets) can be bought using the 'DOT Tickets' smartphone app.

The tourist-saver **Copenhagen Card** (www.copenhagencard.com) includes unlimited public transport throughout the greater region of Copenhagen (including the airport).

times (7am to 9pm and 3.30pm to 5.30pm) and around every 10 minutes at other times.

○ S-buses (buses with an 'S' after their route number) run every five to 10 minutes in peak times and around every 20 minutes at other times. S-buses have fewer stops than A-buses and usually run between 6pm and 1am.

○ Night buses (marked with an 'N' after their route number) run between 1am and 5am.

○ The free Copenhagen city maps at the tourist office show bus routes and are very useful.

Metro

○ Consists of four lines: M1 (green), M2 (yellow) , M3 (red) and M4 (blue). An M4 extension is due for completion in 2024.

○ Metro trains run around the clock, with a frequency of two to four minutes in peak times, three to six minutes during the day and on weekends, and seven to 20 minutes at night.

○ All four lines connect at Kongens Nytorv. The M1, M2 and M3 lines also connect at Frederiksberg. The M1 and M2 lines also connect at Christianshavn, Nørreport and Forum.

○ The M3 line reaches Central Station. The M2 line reaches the airport.

○ The rechargeable Rejsekort travel card is valid on the metro.

○ See www.m.dk for more information.

Bicycle

○ The city-wide rental system **Bycyklen** (City Bikes; www.bycyklen.dk/ en/about-bycyklen; per hr 30kr) offers high-tech 'Smart Bikes' with GPS, multispeed electric motors and locks. The bikes must by paid for by credit card via the website or the bike's touchscreen.

○ Bikes can be carried free on S-trains, but are banned at Nørreport station on weekdays between 7am and 8.30am and between 3.30pm and 5pm. Enter train carriages with the large white bicycle graphic on the windows. Keep your bike behind the line in the designated bicycle area. Stay with the bike at all times.

○ Bikes can be carried on the metro (except from 7am to 9am and from 3.30pm to 5.30pm on weekdays). Bike tickets (13kr) are required on metro and city bus services. Purchase bike tickets at metro and S-train stations or using the 'DOT Tickets' app.

Train

○ Known locally as S-tog, Copenhagen's suburban train network runs seven lines through Central Station (København H). The S-train runs between Copenhagen Airport and Central Station.

○ Services run every four to 20 minutes from approximately 5am to 12.30am. All-night services run hourly on Friday and Saturday (half-hourly on line F).

○ The rechargeable Rejsekort travel card is valid on S-train services.

Boat

○ Movia operates the city's yellow commuter ferries, known as Harbour Buses.

○ Route 991 runs south along the harbour, 992 runs north. There are eight harbour stops, including Det Kongelige Bibliotek (Royal Library), Nyhavn and Operaen (Opera House).

○ Route 993 serves as a shuttle service between Nyhavn and Operaen.

○ The rechargeable Rejsekort travel card is valid on Harbour Buses.

Essential Information

Accessible Travel

○ Copenhagen, and Denmark in general, are improving accessibility all the time, although accessibility is not ubiquitous. The official www.visitcopenhagen.com website lists accessible attractions, stations, hotels and hostels, as

well as practical tips and useful links. Click on 'Planning', then 'Accessible Copenhagen'.

○ Download Lonely Planet's free Guide to Accessible Travel at https://shop.lonely planet.com/categories/accessible-travel.com.

○ Useful resource **God Adgang** (Good Access; www.godadgang.dk) lists service providers who have had their facilities registered and labelled for accessibility.

Business Hours

Opening hours vary throughout the year. We've provided high-season opening hours; hours generally decrease in the shoulder and low seasons.

Banks 10am–4pm Monday to Friday (to 5.30pm or 6pm Thursday)

Bars 4pm–midnight, to 2am or later Friday and Saturday (clubs on weekends may open until 5am)

Boutiques 10am or 11am–6pm Monday to Friday, to 4pm Saturday, some open Sunday

Cafes 8am–5pm or 6pm

Money-Saving Tips

○ Some museums offer free entry, either daily or once weekly.

○ Seniors and students qualify for discounts on some transport fares and museum entry. You'll need to show proof of student status or age.

○ Self-catering at supermarkets and markets can help keep food costs down.

○ Consider getting around on foot – compact Copenhagen was made for walking.

Department stores 10am–8pm

Restaurants noon–10pm or 11pm

Supermarkets 8am–9pm or 10pm (some open 7am, a few open 24 hours)

Covid-19

Check https://en.coronasmitte.dk/travel-rules for the latest government guidelines, restrictions and entry requirements.

Discount Cards

Copenhagen Card (www.copenhagencard.com) gives you access to over 80 museums and attractions, as well as free public transport. Each adult card includes up to two children aged under 10. The card can

be bought online, at the Copenhagen Visitors Centre, as well as at the airport information desk, Central Station tourist information centre and at various hotels and 7-Eleven stores.

Electricity

Type C
220V/50Hz

Money

Credit Cards

○ Visa and MasterCard are widely accepted in Denmark (American Express and Diners Club less so).

○ In many places (hotels, petrol stations, restaurants, shops) a surcharge may be imposed on foreign cards (up to 3.75%). If there is a surcharge, it must be advertised (eg on the menu, at reception).

Public Holidays

New Year's Day (Nytårsdag) 1 January

Maundy Thursday (Skærtorsdag) Thursday before Easter

Good Friday (Langfredag) Friday before Easter

Easter Day (Påskedag) Sunday in March or April

Easter Monday (2 påskedag) Day after Easter

Great Prayer Day (Stor Bededag) Fourth Friday after Easter

Ascension Day (Kristi Himmelfartsdag) Sixth Thursday after Easter

Whitsunday
(Pinsedag) Seventh Sunday after Easter

Whitmonday
(2 pinsedag) Seventh Monday after Easter

Constitution Day
(Grundlovsdag) 5 June

Christmas Eve
(Juleaften) 24 December (from noon)

Christmas Day
(Juledag) 25 December

Boxing Day (2 juledag) 26 December

Safe Travel

Copenhagen is a very safe city, but you should always employ common sense.

o Keep your belongings in sight, particularly in busy places.

o Keep clear of the busy bike lanes that run beside roads; they are easy to wander onto (and straight into the path of cyclists).

Toilets

o Public toilets are generally easy to find and most are free to use.

o Department stores, libraries and major train stations have toilets.

Dos & Don'ts

o **Cycling rules** Brush up on cycling rules *before* you start pedalling.

o **Crossing the street** Wait for the pedestrian light to turn green, even if the road is clear.

o **Punctuality** Trains and tours run on time. Danes operate similarly in social situations.

o **Swimming** Don't swim in canals other than the designated Harbour Baths.

o **Queuing** Machines dispensing numbered tickets are common at places where queues might form. Grab a ticket and wait your turn.

o **Toasts** Raise your glass, say *skål* (cheers!) and make eye contact with everyone.

o Museums, cafes and restaurants have toilets for guests.

Tourist Information

Copenhagen Visitors Centre (www.visitcopenhagen.com) Copenhagen's excellent and informative information centre has a cafe and lounge with free wi-fi; it also sells the Copenhagen Card.

Visas

EU & Schengen countries No visa required.

UK, USA, Canada, Australia, New

Zealand, most Latin American and some Asian countries No visa required for tourist stays of less than 90 days. From 1 January 2023, nationals of these countries will require pre-authorisation to enter Denmark under the new European Travel Information and Authorisation System (ETIAS; www.etias.com).

Other countries Citizens of many African and some Latin American, Asian and former Soviet bloc countries require a visa; see www.nyidanmark.dk.

Language

Most of the sounds in Danish have equivalents in English, and by reading our pronunciation guides as if they were English, you're sure to be understood. There are short and long versions of each vowel, and additional 'combined vowels' or diphthongs. Consonants can be 'swallowed' and even omitted completely, creating (together with vowels) a glottal stop or *stød steudh* which sounds rather like the Cockney pronunciation of the 'tt' in 'bottle'. Note that *ai* is pronounced as in 'aisle', *aw* as in 'saw', *eu* as the 'u' in 'nurse', *ew* as the 'ee' in 'see' with rounded lips, *ow* as in 'how', *dh* as the 'th' in 'that', and *r* is trilled. The stressed syllables are in italics in our pronunciation guides.

To enhance your trip with a phrasebook, visit **lonelyplanet.com**.

Basics

Hello.
Goddag.   go·da

Goodbye.
Farvel.   faar·*vel*

Yes./No.
Ja./Nej.   ya/nai

Please.
Vær så venlig.   ver saw *ven*·lee

Thank you.
Tak.   taak

You're welcome.
Selv tak.   sel taak

Excuse me.
Undskyld mig.   awn·skewl mai

Sorry.
Undskyld.   awn·skewl

How are you?
Hvordan går det?   vor·*dan* gawr dey

Good, thanks.
Godt, tak.   got taak

What's your name?
Hvad hedder du?   va *hey*·dha doo

My name is ...
Mit navn er ...   mit nown ir ...

Do you speak English?
Taler du engelsk?   ta·la dee/doo eng·elsk

I don't understand.
Jeg forstår ikke.   yai for·*stawr* i·ke

Eating & Drinking

What would you recommend?
Hvad du anbefale?   va doo an·*bey*·fa·le

Do you have vegetarian food?
Har I vegetarmad?   haar ee vey·ge·*taar*·madh

Cheers!
Skål!   skawl

I'd like (the) ..., please.
Jeg vil gerne have ..., tak.   yai vil *gir*·ne ha ... taak

   bill
   regningen   *rai*·ning·en

Emergencies

Help!
Hjælp!   yelp

Go away!
Gå væk!   gaw vek

Call ...!
Ring efter ...!   ring ef·ta ...

  a doctor
  en læge   in le·ye

  the police
  politiet   poh·lee·tee·et

It's an emergency!
Det er et   dey ir it
nødstilfælde!   neudhs·til·fe·le

I'm lost.
Jeg er faret vild.   yai ir faa·ret veel

I'm sick.
Jeg er syg.   yai ir sew

It hurts here.
Det gør ondt her.   dey geur awnt heyr

I'm allergic to...
Jeg er allergisk   yai ir a·ler·geesk
over for...   o·va for...

Where's the toilet?
Hvor er toilettet?   vor ir toy·le·tet

Shopping & Services

I'm looking for ...
Jeg leder efter ...   yai li·dha ef·ta ...

How much is it?
Hvor meget   vor maa·yet
koster det?   kos·ta dey

Can I have a look?
Må jeg se?   maw yai sey

Time & Numbers

What time is it?
Hvad er klokken?   va ir klo·ken

1	*en*	in
2	*to*	toh
3	*tre*	trey
4	*fire*	feer
5	*fem*	fem
6	*seks*	seks
7	*syv*	sew
8	*otte*	aw·te
9	*ni*	nee
10	*ti*	tee
100	*hundrede*	hoon·re·dhe
1000	*tusind*	too·sen

Transport & Directions

Where's the ...?
Hvor er ...?   vor ir ...

What's the address?
Hvad er adressen?   va ir a·draa·sen

How do I get there?
Hvordan kommer   vor·dan ko·ma
jeg derhen?   yai deyr·hen

Please take me to (this address).
Vær venlig at   ver ven·lee at
køre mig   keu·re mai
til (denne adresse).   til (de·ne a·draa·se)

Please stop here.
Venligst stop her.   ven·leest stop heyr

boat	*båden*	baw·dhen
bicycle	*cykel*	see·kel
bus	*bussen*	boo·sen
plane	*flyet*	flew·et
train	*toget*	taw·et

Behind the Scenes

Send Us Your Feedback

We love to hear from travellers – your comments help make our books better. We read every word, and we guarantee that your feedback goes straight to the authors. Visit lonelyplanet.com/contact to submit your updates and suggestions.

Note: We may edit, reproduce and incorporate your comments in Lonely Planet products such as guidebooks, websites and digital products, so let us know if you are happy to have your name acknowledged. For a copy of our privacy policy visit lonelyplanet.com/legal.

Abigail's Thanks

Tak to everyone who helped me: Gareth and Lotte; Luca, Gabriel, Jack, Vale: Mikkel Ustrup and Justina Mørup at Tivoli; Nikolina Olsen-Rule at Danmark Designmuseum; Egill Bjarnason and Sasha Drew.

Egill's Thanks

Thanks to Anne-Katrine Frøster Karmann, Pål Øivind Christiansen, Jan M. Olsen, Jan Hybertz Gøricke, Karina Bach-Lauritsen, Einar Teitur, Mariana Garcia, Muyingo Siraj, Amanda Bomholt, Cecilie Gundersen, Carolyn Bain, Lars Jensen, Mikkel Staun Poulsen, Mette Larsen, Bjarni Hardarson, Elin Gunnlaugsdottir, Amanda Bomholt, Kaj Ravn, Aðalgeir Bjarnason, Jónína Hermanns-dóttir, Sigrún Sæta.

Acknowledgements

Cover photograph: Superkilen park Phoenixproduction/Shutterstock© Back cover: Danish pastries, Oleksandr Berezko/Shutterstock© Photographs p36-7 (clockwise from bottom left): Oliver Foerstner, TMA Harding, Jaroslav Moravcik,Oliver Foerstner, all Shutterstock© Photograph p83: Nikolina Olsen-Rule: Luka Hesselberg-Thomsen

This Book

This 6th edition of Lonely Planet's Pocket Copenhagen guidebook was researched and written by Egill Bjarnason and Abigail Blasi. The previous edition was written by Cristian Bonetto. This guidebook was produced by the following:

Senior Product Editor
Sasha Drew

Cartographer
Hunor Csutoros

Product Editor
Sarah Farrell

Book Designer
Fabrice Robin

Assisting Editor
Kellie Langdon

Cover Researcher
Gwen Cotter

Thanks to Amanda Bomholt, Melanie Dankel, Bruce Evans, Nikolina Olsen-Rule, Fionnuala Twomey, Mikkel Ustrup

Index

See also separate subindexes for:

- ✪ **Eating p157**
- ● **Drinking p158**
- ✪ **Entertainment p158**
- 🛍 **Shopping p158**